T. Lansing Davies

Facts in Civil Government

paragraphed and alphabetically arranged with cross references, for the teacher,

the student, and the citizen

T. Lansing Davies

Facts in Civil Government
paragraphed and alphabetically arranged with cross references, for the teacher, the student, and the citizen

ISBN/EAN: 9783337255268

Printed in Europe, USA, Canada, Australia, Japan

Cover: Foto ©Suzi / pixelio.de

More available books at **www.hansebooks.com**

FACTS

IN

CIVIL GOVERNMENT

PARAGRAPHED AND ALPHABETICALLY
ARRANGED WITH CROSS-
REFERENCES

FOR
THE TEACHER THE STUDENT
AND
THE CITIZEN

BY

T. L. DAVIES, A. B.

Principal Spencer Normal School, and Ex-Member West Virginia
State Legislature

"Thou too, sail on, O Ship of State!
Sail on, O Union, strong and great!"

SPENCER, W. VA.
GEM PUBLISHING CO.
1899

TO THE

Army of Pupils

WITH WHOM, IN THE PAST NINETEEN YEARS, HE
HAS BEEN MOST PLEASANTLY ASSOCIATED
IN THE SCHOOLROOM, AND AT THE
REQUEST OF MANY OF WHOM
IT IS NOW SENT FORTH.

This Volume,

THE CONTENTS OF WHICH
THEY HAVE KINDLY COMMENDED
IN THEIR CLASS WORK, AND TO WHOM
MUCH OF IT WILL BE FAMILIAR AND WILL SERVE
AS A REMINDER OF OTHER DAYS, IS RESPECTFUL-
LY DEDICATED BY THEIR WELL-WISHING FRIEND,

THE AUTHOR.

tion in the *minimum space.* In this respect, the busy knowledge-seeker is invited to compare this little book with other more pretentious volumes on the same subject.

It is confidently believed that the teacher preparing for examination, will find in this little volume, a trusty friend whose thorough acquaintance will enable him to pass any examination on the subject in hand; that the student will find the study of Civil Government more interesting if he keeps it within easy reach, no matter what text book he may be studying; and that the citizen will find it useful for reference.

Since "to err is human," it is not necessary to remark that the author does not regard this little work as absolutely perfect. If it were, it would be lonely indeed.

The author acknowledges obligations to W. L. STARKEY, Esq., of the Spencer Bar, for valuable suggestions and aid in the preparation of the following pages.

Independence Day, 1899.

FACTS

IN

Civil Government

NOTE I—*Parenthetical numbers in the text refer to other sections where information may be found on the subjects preceding them; thus, (549) in the first section, refers to NEGOTIABLE in the text. Where the information is not required, disregard the references.*

NOTE II—*At the close of the book, will be found an alphabetical index of subjects treated of in SUB-TOPICS or under different titles. If the subject desired is not found as a leading topic look in the index.*

GOVERNMENT.—Controlling power; the power that makes, interprets and executes the laws; the power that rules a body politic.

CIVIL GOVERNMENT.—The power by which a body politic controls its citizens in their relations to each other and to the state.

---

1. Acceptance.—An agreement to pay a draft, bill of exchange, or order, when due.

2. The person accepting, writes "*Accepted*," with his name, across the face of the paper; it then becomes negotiable (**549**).

2. Accessory.—One who advises, commands, or otherwise aids in the commission of a crime at which he is not present.

2. An *accessory before the fact* is one who advises or commands the commission of a crime.

3. An *accessory after the fact* is one who knowingly conceals the offender or aids him to escape punishment.

3. Accidental Presidents.—Those who succeed to the presidency by the death of the President.

2. Thus far, they are Tyler, Fillmore, Johnson and Arthur.

4. Acclamation, Vote by.—A vote taken by those in favor of a question saying together; "*Aye;*" and those opposed, "*No.*"

5. Accommodation Paper.—A draft accepted, or a note given, without consideration, merely as an accommodation, for the purpose of raising money on credit.

6. Accomplice.—An associate in the commission of a crime, either as a principal or as an accessory (**2**).

7. Account Current.—A running account between two persons or firms, or an itemized statement of the same.

8. Account Sales.—An itemized statement of sales and expenses made by a commission merchant to his principal.

9. Acknowledgment.—The declaration of one's own act before a proper officer, to make it legally valid.

10. Act.—A law passed by a legislative body.

11. Administrator.—A man duly appointed by the proper authority, to manage and distribute the estate of a person dying intestate (432), or in whose will no competent executor (326) is named.

2. An administrator is appointed by a court, while an executor is appointed by the deceased himself in his will. Their duties are the same.

12. Administratrix.—Feminine of administrator (11).

13. Admiral.—The chief officer of a fleet. The highest rank of naval officers.

2. There are three grades, viz., Admiral, Vice Admiral and Rear Admiral.

3. An Admiral is of equal rank with a General in the army.

4. The office of Admiral, retired in 1890, was revived in 1899, to compliment Admiral Dewey.

14. Admiralty Court.—A court that interprets and applies maritime law (499).

2. In the United States, there are no special Admiralty Courts; here, admiralty jurisdiction (15) is vested in the United States District Courts, with an appeal to the higher courts.

15. Admiralty and Maritime Jurisdiction.—Jurisdiction over cases arising on the sea, lakes and navigable rivers.

2. These cases include questions relating to ships, crimes committed on the high seas, (390) collisions, prizes of war (641), maritime contracts, and questions pertaining to navigation generally.

3. The United States District Court has exclusive original jurisdiction (451, 2) in such

cases, with an appeal to the higher courts.

16. Admission of New States.—New States are usually formed by act of Congress, from Territories.

2. For admission into the Union as a new State, there is no definite requirement as to population.

3. When a Territory seeks admission into the Union, Congress passes an *Enabling Act* (**311**) authorizing the people of the Territory to frame and adopt a State constitution in harmony with the United States Constitution. When this is done, Congress passes another act admitting it.

4. The enabling act sometimes provides for the admission of a new State on proclamation of the President alone.

5. The people of a Territory may frame a State constitution before they petition for admission as a State, and may be admitted by Congress without an enabling act. Several Territories have done this.

6. No State can be divided into two or more new States without the consent of the Legislature of the State concerned, and of Congress.

7. No new State can be formed from parts of two or more States without the consent of such States and of Congress.

8. Two or more States can not be united to form one new State without the consent of the States concerned and of Congress.

9. Of the forty-five States, (1899), thirteen were the original States; twenty-six were

formed from organized Territories; one (California) never had a territorial government; one (Texas) was annexed, and four (Vermont, Maine, Kentucky, and West Virginia) were formed from other States.

17. Affiant.—One who makes an affidavit.

18. Affidavit.—A statement or declaration in writing, signed and sworn to before an officer authorized to administer oaths.

2. An affidavit differs from a deposition (**276**) in that the affiant (**17**) is not cross-examined.

19. Affirmation.—A solemn declaration with an appeal to God for the truth of what is affirmed, made by one who is conscientiously unwilling to take an oath, to which it is equivalent in law.

20. Agent.—A person authorized to act for another, called the principal, in dealing with third parties.

21. Albany Regency.—A combination of politicians that manipulated the Democratic party in New York from 1820 to 1854. Martin Van Buren, Wm. L. Marcey and Benjamin F. Butler were leading members.

2. It took its name from its location at Albany, the State Capital.

22. Alien.—A foreigner. A subject of a foreign country. One owing allegiance (**24**) to another country.

2. His rights differ in different States.

3. In some States he cannot hold real estate.

4. He can vote in about one-third of the States.

5. He cannot hold office in any State.

2

23. Alien and Sedition Laws.—Acts passed by Congress in 1798, during hostile relations with France, and expiring by limitation in 1800 and 1801 respectively. They were bitterly opposed.

2. The *Alien Law* authorized the President to banish any alien whose influence he might consider dangerous to the country. It was never enforced.

3. The *Sedition Law* provided fines and imprisonment for those who should speak, write, or publish any false or malicious things against the President, Congress, or the government. It was enforced in several instances.

24. Allegiance.—The duty or obligation that a subject (**778**) owes to his sovereign (**746**) or government (**379**).

25. Alliance.—A union, as between States.

2. The Constitution forbids States from forming any alliances.

26. Alternate Delegate.—A person selected to attend a convention and to act in the place of a regular delegate should he be absent.

27. Ambassador.—The highest rank of foreign representatives of a country (**283**).

28. Amnesty.—A general pardon granted by the goverment to subjects previously engaged in insurrection (**426**), rebellion (**668**), etc.

29. Anarchy.—A total absence of all government and law.

30. "Another County Heard From."—A phrase that originated in 1876, when the presidential election returns came in very slowly from the doubtful States.

31. Appeal.—The removing of a case from a

lower to a higher court for a rehearing or a review.

2. An appeal carries both the law and the facts of the case to the higher court.

32. Appellant.—One who appeals a case from a lower to a higher court.

33. Appellate Jurisdiction.—The right of a court to review cases appealed to it from a lower court.

34. Appellee.—The defendant in an appealed case; one whose case is appealed to a higher court by his opponent, the appellant(32).

35. Appointive Office.—An office to be filled by appointment.

36. Appointments, U. S.—All United States officers except the President and Vice-President are appointed in some way.

2. Senators and Representatives are not United States *officers*, but *representatives* of the States and of the people respectively.

37. Apportionment of U. S. Representatives.—The assignment of Representatives to the different States according to population.

2. A new apportionment is made every ten years, and goes into effect the third year after the census is taken and continues ten years.

3. Congress first decides the number of Representatives to be elected. The total population of all the States (the Territories and the District of Columbia are not included) is then divided by this number. The quotient is the ratio of representation.

4. The population of each State is then divided by this ratio, and the quotient, exclu-

sive of any remainder, gives its number of Representatives.

5. To the States having the largest remainders, Congress then assigns one additional member each, until the number fixed upon is obtained.

6. The present (1899) ratio of representation is 173,901.

7. The only restriction that the Constitution places on the number of Representatives is that the number must not exceed one for every 30,000 inhabitants.

38. Appurtenance.—Something naturally belonging to, and going with, something else; as buildings that belong to the land on which they stand.

39. Arbitration.—The method of settling disputes between parties by referring the matters in controversy to disinterested parties chosen by the disputants, for judgment.

2. Several States provide for courts of arbitration for those who prefer them to courts of law.

3. Arbitration is becoming a popular method of settling disputes between civilized nations.

4. Criminal cases can not be settled by arbitration.

5. The decision of the arbitrators is called an *award*.

40. Archives, U. S.—The place where the original copies of national laws, treaties, and public records are kept. The Secretary of State has charge of it.

41. Armed Neutrality.—An alliance formed in 1780-82, by most countries of Europe, and the United States, to protect themselves against British depredations on neutral commerce.

42. Armistice.—A temporary suspension of hostilities, by mutual agreement, between two nations at war, or between two armies. A truce (**820**).

43. Armory.—A place where fire arms are stored or manufactured.

44. Army.—An organized body armed for war.

2. A *standing* or *regular army* is a permanent, organized body of professional soldiers.

3. Congress can not make appropriations for the standing army for longer than two years at a time; but it can do so for the n

4. The United States standing army numbers 2,179 officers and 25,353 privates; total, 27,532.

5. The President is Commander-in-Chief (**179**) of the United States army.

6. The United States is divided into eight military departments or districts.

7. An army officer can be dismissed only on the sentence of a court martial (**240**).

8. Army regulations are made by Congress.

45. Army and Navy Officers.—Following are the army and navy officers of corresponding grades, with salaries:

Army Officers.	*Navy Officers.*
GENERAL, retired, $13,500.	ADMIRAL, $13,000.
LIEUTENANT-GENERAL, retired, $11,000.	VICE-ADMIRAL, retired, $9,000.

MAJOR-GENERAL, $7,500.	REAR ADMIRAL, $6,000.
BRIGADIER-GENERAL, $5,500.	COMMODORE, $5,000.
COLONEL, $3,500 to $4,500.	CAPTAIN, $4,500.
LIEUTENANT-COLONEL, $3,000 to $4,000.	COMMANDER, $3,500
MAJOR, $2,500 to $3,500.	LIEUTENANT-COMMANDER, $2,800,
CAPTAIN, $1,800 to $2,800.	LIEUTENANT, $2,400 to $2,600.
FIRST LIEUTENANT, $1,500 to $2,240.	MASTER, $1,800 to $2,000.
SECOND LIEUTENANT, $1,400 to $2,100.	ENSIGN, $1,200 to $1,400.

46. Army Divisions and Commands.—Following are the regular divisions of the army; but the figures represent averages, and are subject to change:

(*1*) An army, three corps.

(*2*) A corps, three divisions.

(*3*) A division, three brigades.

(*4*) A brigade, three regiments.

(*5*) A regiment, three battalions.

(*6*) A battalion, three companies.

(*7*) A company, one hundred men.

2. Officers command forces as follows:

(*1*) Major General, a corps or division.

(*2*) Brigadier General, a brigade or division.

(*3*) Colonel, a regiment.

(*4*) Major, a battalion.

(*5*) Captain, a company.

3. A Lieutenant-Colonel is a Vice-Colonel; that is, he takes the place of his superior when the latter is absent.

4. The Adjutant and Quartermaster rank as Lieutenants, and are appointed by the Colonel.

5. The Surgeon ranks as Major.

6. The Assistant Surgeon and Chaplain rank as Captains.

47. Arraignment.—The act of producing a prisoner before a court to answer to an indictment or a complaint.

48. Arrest.—The seizing a person by an officer, and detaining him in the custody of the law. (*Freedom from*, **201**, 14).

49. Arrest of Judgment.—The staying a judgment, for legal cause, after the verdict is rendered.

50. Arsenal.—A place where war equipments are manufactured or stored.

51. Arson.—The malicious burning of a dwelling or other building belonging to another.

2. To burn an inhabited dwelling in the night time, is arson in the first degree, and is, in some States, punishable by death.

52. Articles of Confederation.—The first compact, or constitution, made by the original thirteen States for their government.

2. It was adopted by the Continental Congress (**222**), November 15, 1777, and ratified by the States March 1, 1781, when it went into effect, and remained the supreme law of the States until March 4, 1789.

3. The Articles were *thirteen* in number.

4. The principal features of the Articles of Confederation may be summed up as follows:

(*1*) The *unanimous ratification of the States* was necessary to make them binding.

(*2*) The *unanimous vote of the States* was

necessary to amend them. Three times, amendments were defeated by one State.

(*3*) The concurrence of *nine States* was necessary in all important measures.

(*4*) Congress consisted of but *one House*.

(*5*) There was *no Executive* (**323**) and *no Judiciary* (**449**)—only a legislative body.

(*6*) Each State was represented by not fewer than *two*, nor more than *seven* delegates.

(*7*) Congress could appoint a "*Committee of States*," consisting of one delegate from each State, to act when that body was not in session.

(*8*) Each State had but *one vote* in Congress. If a State were not represented by at least two delegates, or if an even number of its delegates voted for and against a question, that State *lost its vote*.

(*9*) Each State paid its own delegates.

(*10*) All international questions, treaties, etc., were in the hands of Congress.

(*11*) The *States* could impose duties (**296**) and imposts (**408**).

(*12*) Each State retained its independent sovereignty.

(*13*) The national revenue was to be raised by the several States, the amount being apportioned among them respectively in proportion to their *wealth*; but *no State could be compelled to pay its share*.

(*14*) The Confederation was a *league of States;* not a union of the people.

(*15*) Congress could *advise*, but not *enforce* measures.

5. In discussing the defects of the Articles of Confederation, a writer, as early as 1786, well said: "By this political compact, the United States in Congress have exclusive power-for the following purposes, without being able to execute one of them:

(1) "They may make and conclude treaties, but can only recommend the observance of them.

(2) "They may appoint ambassadors (27), but can not defray even the expenses of their tables.

(3) "They may borrow money in their own name on the faith of the Union, but can not pay a dollar.

(4) "They may coin money, but can not buy an ounce of bullion.

(5) "They may make war, and determine what number of troops are necessary, but they can not raise a single soldier.

(6) "In short, they may *declare everything*, but *do nothing*."

6. "They were a rope of sand which could bind no one."—Wilson's *The State*, p. 471.

7. To the patent weakness of the Articles of Confederation, we owe the wonderful strength of our Constitution.

53. Artificial or Ficticious Person.—A corporation (232) or body politic (94), as distinguished from a natural person.

54. Artillery.—The soldiers that manipulate cannon and other heavy guns. Heavy arms.

55. Assessments, P o l i t i c a l.—Contributions levied upon candidates and office holders by committees to defray campaign expenses.

56. Assessor.—One who lists persons and the value of property for the purpose of taxation.

57. Assignee.—(*a*) A person to whom the property of a bankrupt is transferred for the benefit of his creditors.

(*b*) One to whom a note, bond, lease, or other interest is transferred by writing.

58. Assignment.—(*a*) The transfer of a bankrupt's property to an assignee (**57**) for the benefit of creditors.

(*b*) The transfer of any title or interest in property to another by writing.

59. Assignor.—One who makes an assignment (**58**).

60. Attachment.—A writ ordering an officer to take the property of a debtor into custody pending the hearing of a case, when such a course is necessary to keep the creditors from being defrauded.

61. Attainder.—The extinction of the civil rights and privileges of a person, and the confiscation (**200**) of his property to the government. (*Bill of,* **80**).

62. Attorney.—One legally appointed to act for another, is an *attorney in fact.*

2. One skilled in law who acts for clients in legal matters, is an *attorney-at-law.*

63. Auditor.—A person who adjusts and examines into the validity and correctness of accounts.

2. There are six auditors of the United States Treasury.

64. Australian Ballot System.—A system of

voting that provides booths at each voting
place, in which all voters prepare their ballots
in secret.

2. The ballots are printed at public expense,
and distributed by sworn officers.

3. All ballots must be accounted for, and
none must be taken from the voting room.

4. If a ballot is spoiled in marking, it must
be returned to the officers before another can
be obtained from the clerk.

5. Except the election officers, no person is
permitted to approach within a certain distance of the polls, except to vote.

6. Two forms of ballots are used; namely,
the *"blanket ballot"* and the *"individual ballot."*

7. The blanket ballot contains, on one sheet,
the names of all the candidates regularly nominated by all parties, and the voter indicates
his choice by marking as required by the law
of the State in which he votes. This form of
ballot is generally used.

8. The individual ballot system provides a
a separate ticket for each party. This form
of ballot is used in New York.

9. None but official ballots must be used.

10. Sworn officers aid the blind, the sick and
the maimed, to prepare their ballots.

11. There are two methods of arranging the
names of candidates on the ticket—

(a) The Australian method arranges the
names of all candidates for a given office alphabetically in one group, with or without
their party connections being given.

(*b*) The other method groups all offices and names of candidates *by parties.*

12. The system was originated by Francis S. Dutton, in South Australia, in 1857.

13. It was introduced in the United States (Massachusetts) in 1888.

14. It is now used generally throughout the United States, Europe, and Canada.

65. Autocrat.—An absolute ruler; a despot.

66. Autonomy.—Political independence; the power or right of a nation, state, city or other body, to govern itself.

67. Bail—(*a*) Security for the appearance of a prisoner in court for trial, given for the purpose of securing his release.

(*b*) The person or persons who go on the prisoner's bond. The bondsmen may have the prisoner re-arrested in any State or at any time.

2. Excessive bail is prohibited by the Constitution.

68. Balance of Power.—An adjustment of power by which a nation, state, or party, is able to control the relations between other nations, states, or parties.

69. Balance of Trade.—The difference between the money value of the exports and imports of a country.

70. Ballot.—(*a*) A written or printed ticket or other device used to enable one to vote secretly.

(*b*) The act of voting by ballot.

(*c*) The whole number of votes cast in an election.

71. Ballot Box.— A box in which votes are deposited at the polls.

72. Bank of the United States.— The first charter was issued in 1791 and expired in 1811.

2. The second charter extended from 1816 to 1836.

3. A bill to re-charter the bank a second time was passed by Congress in 1832, but was vetoed by President Jackson.

73. Bankrupt Law.— A law that releases a bankrupt or a debtor who can not pay his debts, from all obligations, on giving up all his property (except what is legally exempted), to be distributed among his creditors.

2. The Constitution gives Congress power to establish uniform bankrupt laws.

3. Such laws have been in force as follows: 1800-1803, 1841-1843, 1867-1878, and the present law of 1898.

4. When Congress fails to provide such a law, the States may do so, but their laws must yield to the acts of Congress when passed.

5. The U. S. District Courts, the Supreme Court of the District of Columbia, the District Courts of the Territories, and the U. S. Courts of Indian Territory and Alaska, are designated as *Courts of Bankruptcy*, with appeal through the higher courts to the United States Supreme Court.

6. A bankrupt is entitled to the benefit of the exemption allowed by his State.

74. Bar'l (barrel).—A slang expression referring to the money used by a candidate in a campaign.

75. Barter.—A trade; a mere exchange of goods.

76. Belligerent.— A nation actually waging war against another nation.

77. Bicameral.— Having two branches; as our bicameral Congress and Legislatures.

78. Bigamy.— The offense of marrying a second wife or husband while a first legal wife or husband is still living.

79. Bill.—A form or draft of a proposed law submitted to a legislative body for enactment, but not yet made law.

2. A bill has three parts—

(*1*) The title,

(*2*) The enacting clause (**312**),

(*3*) The body of the bill.

3. All revenue bills (**696**) must originate in the House of Representatives, but the Senate may propose and concur in amendments.

4. In some, but not in all States, also, revenue bills must originate in the House.

5. Any other bill may originate in either house.

6. A bill may become a law by passing both houses of Congress and then—

(*1*) Being signed by the President, or

(*2*) Not being returned by the President within ten days (Sundays excepted) unless Congress adjourn earlier, or

(*3*) Being passed by a two-thirds vote over his veto.

7. A bill may fail

(*1*) To pass the House, or

(*2*) To pass the Senate, or

(*3*) To be signed by the President, or

(*4*) To be held ten days by him, Congress adjourning sooner, or

(*5*) To be passed over his veto.

8. A majority vote is necessary to pass a bill.

9. A bill may be introduced—

(*1*) By a member;

(*2*) By a committee; or

(*3*) By the house.

10. When introduced, a bill is referred to a committee for critical consideration, which committee returns it with or without recommendation as to its enactment.

11. A bill must be read three times in each house, on three different days, except by unanimous consent, when it can be disposed of at once.

12. A bill may be read in three ways:

(*1*) By reading the title,

(*2*) By reading the enacting clause (**312**) or

(*3*) By reading the entire bill, section by section.

13. A bill is read the first time for information; on the second reading, it is discussed and amended, and on the third reading it is passed or rejected.

14. No amendments, except to fill blanks, are in order on the third reading, without unanimous consent.

15. Before a bill is passed on the third reading, it is engrossed, or copied in a plain hand with all its amendments, on parchment.

16. When a bill passes one house, it is sent to the other, where it is acted upon as if it were

an original bill; and when thus acted upon, it is sent back to the house where it originated.

17. When a bill is passed in both houses, the Clerk of the house in which it originated, delivers it to the Executive (**323**) for his signature, except in States where the Governor has no veto power (**335,4**), when it becomes a law.

80. Bill of Attainder.— A special legislative act inflicting death, without due process of law, upon persons supposed to be guilty of high crimes.

2. Congress and the States are prohibited by the Constitution, from passing any bill of attainder, which is held to include also the Bill of Pains and Penalties (**83**).

81. Bills of Credit.— Paper money; as U. S Treasury notes, or paper obligations issued by a State on its own faith and credit, and designed to circulate as ordinary money.

2. States are prohibited from issuing bills of credit.

3. State bonds and bank notes are not bills of credit.

4. Until 1863, State banks were chartered, which issued paper money that people could accept or reject as they chose; but the government has taxed these bills out of existence.

82. Bill of Indictment.—A written accusation against a party, regularly drawn up by the prosecuting officer, and presented to the grand jury (**383**) for investigation.

83. Bill of Pains and Penalties.— The same

as bill of attainder (.80), except that the punishment is less than death.

84. Bill of Rights.— A formal declaration of rights and privileges reserved to the people.

2. The first ten Amendments to the Constitution constitute our American Bill of Rights.

3. In general, our Bill of Rights guarantees to the people:

(*1*) Religious freedom;

(*2*) Freedom of speech;

(*3*) Freedom of the press;

(*4*) The right of assembly and petition;

(*5*) The right to keep and bear arms;

(*6*) Exemption from quartering soldiers;

(*7*) Security from unlawful search and seizure;

(*8*) Security in life, liberty and property;

(*9*) Impartial justice and a speedy public trial by jury.

(*10*) Exemption from excessive bail and from cruel and unusual punishment.

4. Except in the army and navy and during war, a person can not be tried for a crime except on indictment.

5. A person can not be put in jeopardy for the same crime twice, and he must be informed of the accusation against him. He need not testify against himself. He must be supplied with counsel, and his witnesses must be compelled to attend and testify.

6. In civil suits for more than twenty dollars, a jury may be demanded.

7. The Government can not take private property without paying for it.

3

8. The American Bill of Rights is derived mainly from the following English documents: the Magna Charta, 1215; the Petition of Rights, 1628; the Habeas Corpus Act, 1679; and The Bill of Rights, 1689.

85. Bill of Sale.—A written instrument formally conveying the ownership of personal property from one person to another where possession is not taken at the time by the purchaser.

86. Bimetallism.—The legalized use of gold and silver as money-standards of a country, with a fixed legal relative value for the metals.

87. Black Codes.—A phrase applied by the North to severe laws enacted by the seceded States, oppressing the negroes after they had been freed.

88. Blockade.—The closing of an enemy's port by armed vessels, in time of war, in order to make it impossible for the enemy, and unlawful for neutrals, to enter or depart therefrom, the purpose being to cut off all supplies and correspondence, with a view to compel the surrender of the place.

2. In order to make a blockade lawful and binding on neutrals, according to international law—

(*1*) War must actually exist, though not necessarily formally declared; the blockade may be the first act of war.

(*2*) Neutrals must have knowledge of the blockade either by formal notice or by the general notority of the fact.

(3) The blockade must be sustained by sufficient force to make it impossible or dangerous to enter or to leave the port.

3. Neutral vessels in the port at the time the blockade is declared, may leave; but only with such cargoes as they already have on board.

4. If a port be blockaded by sea only, neutrals may lawfully carry on trade with the port by land.

5. *Blockade runners*, neutral vessels attempting to pass the blockade, may be seized, with their cargoes, condemned in a prize court (**642**) and confiscated (**200**).

6. When the blockade is ended, it is said to be *raised*.

7. If the blockading vessels be temporarily carried away by a storm, the fact does not serve to raise the blockade.

8. A *paper blockade* is one that is merely ordered or proclaimed, but which is not and can not be made effective.

89. Bloody Bill.—The name applied in South Carolina, to an act passed by Congress March 2, 1833, to enforce the tariff of 1828 and 1832, which that State had declared null and void. Sometimes it is called the *Force Bill* (**354**).

90. Bloody Shirt, To Wave the.—To revive memories of the Civil War by impassioned allusions for political purposes.

91. Blue Laws.—A code of absurdly severe laws erroneously supposed by some to have been introduced in New Haven, Connecticut, in 1644. Rev. Samuel Peters first wrote them.

in his satirical "History of Connecticut".

92. Board of Aldermen.— The upper branch of a city council, the lower branch being the *Common Council.*

2. In some cities, the Board of Aldermen or the Council alone, constitutes the legislative body.

93. Body of Liberties.—A code of 100 fundamental laws established by the Massachusetts Colony in 1641—the first written laws of the Colony.

94. Body Politic.—An entire nation or state considered as a political organization.

95. Bolter.—One who refuses to support a regular candidate or a measure of his party.

96. Bond.—A written obligation under seal

(*a*) To pay a certain sum of money on or before a certain time, for a valuable consideration, or

(*b*) To pay a certain sum in case of the performance or non-performance of a certain specified act as agreed, but not otherwise; as official bonds, etc.

97. Bond, U. S.—A written obligation of the government to repay borrowed money at or before a fixed time. Bonds are of two kinds:

2. *Registered bonds,*—each bond and the name of its owner is registered in the United States Treasury, thus providing against loss by theft, and

3. *Coupon bonds,* which are not registered, but have interest coupons attached to them.

4. United States bonds are not taxed.

98. Boodle.—Money or some commodity (usually liquor) given for votes or influence in a political campaign (118).

99. Boodler.—A person who sells his vote or political influence for money or other valuable consideration—and then usually sells out to the other fellow.

100. Booth.—A temporary stall into which voters go to prepare their ballots in secret.

101. Booty.—The goods of an enemy captured on land in time of war.

2. Booty belongs to the government and not to the soldiers who capture it.

102. Borough.—An incorporated town or village, with some of the powers of a city.

2. The term is still used in Connecticut, Pennsylvania, New Jersey and Minnesota.

103. Bounty.—A premium offered (a) to induce persons to enlist in the army, or (b) to encourage some industry.

104. Bounty Jumper.—One who enlisted in the Federal army towards the close of the Civil War, for the purpose of obtaining the bounty, and then deserted.

105. Bribery.—The act of influencing voters at elections, or of influencing the official acts of public officers, by means of money or other reward.

106. Brother Jonathan.—A name applied to all the people of the United States.

2. It originated from Washington's reference to Jonathan Trumbull, Govenor of Connecticut, as " Brother Jonathan."

107. Buccaneer.—A sea robber; a pirate.

108. Bulldozing.—A term applied to the intimidation of negroes in the South.

109. Buncombe or Bunkum.—Flattering talk made for effect, for mere show or popularity, or to gain any selfish end.

110. Burden of Proof.—The obligation to prove one's side in a controversy. The burden of proof rests on the affirmative.

111. Bureau.—A sub-department under the control of one of the general departments of government (324); as the *Census Bureau*, the *Pension Bureau*, etc.

2. Some of the departments are divided into a number of bureaus, under the control of a chief officer.

112. Bureaucracy.—A government like France, administered by independent departments or bureaus, as distinguished from one carried on by associated departments like our own (137, 2).

113. Burglary.—The unlawful breaking and entering the dwelling house of another in the night time, with intent to commit crime.

2. Burglary constitutes a felony; the punishment varies in the different States.

114. By-Laws.—Subordinate laws in addition to the constitution of a society or corporation, regulating the affairs of the body.

2. A by-law differs from a constitutional law in that the former may usually be temporarily suspended, while the latter can only be affected by formally amending the constitution itself.

115. Cabal.—An association of persons secretly organized to attain some disreputable private ends by intrigue.

116. Cabinet.—The advisory council of the President.

2. It consists of the heads of the Executive Departments (**324**), to-wit:

(*1*) The Secretary of State,

(*2*) The Secretary of the Treasury,

(*3*) The Secretary of War,

(*4*) The Attorney General,

(*5*) The Post Master General,

(*6*) The Secretary of the Navy,

(*7*) The Secretary of the Interior and

(*8*) The Secretary of Agriculture.

3. The salary of a Cabinet officer is $8,000 per year.

4. The President may require the written opinion of any Cabinet officer on any question pertaining to his office.

5. According to a custom established by President Washington, the President may at any time call his Cabinet together for consultation; but there is no legal provision for such meetings.

6. The Cabinet possesses no legal power as a body; it is merely an advisory council.

7. The Cabinet meetings are secret and their proceedings are not recorded.

8. The President is not bound to regard the opinions of his Cabinet.

9. The Cabinet officers are appointed by the President, and confirmed by the Senate.

10. The first Cabinet consisted of but four members; viz., Thomas Jefferson, Secretary of State; Alexander Hamilton, Secretary of

the Treasury; Gen. Henry Knox, Secretary of
War; and Edmund Randolph, Attorney General.

117. Cadet.—A person training for military
or naval service; as students at West Point
an 1 at Annapolis.

118. Campaign.—(*a*) The struggle between
political parties immediately preceding an
election, in which votes are sought to be won.

(*b*) A distinctly connected series of military
operations forming a fixed period in war.

119. Candidate.—One who puts himself for-
ward as an aspirant, or is nominated by others, for some office or position.

120. Canvassing Votes.—The act of examin-
ing and counting votes, and of certifying the
number received by each candidate.

121. Capias (*Thou mayst take*).—A writ issuing from a court commanding an officer to
arrest a person named therein, that he may
answer a plaintiff, answer to a judgment already pronounced against him, or to an indictment; or that he may give testimony.

122. Capital.—The city in which the seat of
government is located.

123. Capital Offense.—A crime punishable
by death, as treason, piracy, murder, arson
in the first degree (**51,2**), etc.

124. Capital Punishment.—Punishment by
death.

125. Capital, U. S.—Washington, on the Potomac River, in the District of Columbia
(**797,18**).

2. It is under the exclusive control of Con-

gress.

3. The site was selected in 1790, and became the capital in 1800.

4. It was captured by the British and burned in 1814.

5. The idea of having a capital city under direct government control is distinctively American.

126. Capitol.—A state house. The building in which Congress or a State Legislature holds its sessions.

127. Capitulation.—(*a*) The act of surrendering to an enemy on certain prescribed conditions.

(*b*) The instrument setting forth the terms of a surrender.

2. The "*honors of war*" or the privilege of marching out with drums beating and with colors flying is sometimes accorded to the conquered.

128. Capitation Tax.—A poll tax (**618**).

129. Cartel.—An agreement between belligerents for the exchange of prisoners of war.

130. Cartel Ship.—A ship used to convey exchanged prisoners, or to carry propositions to the enemy.

131. Castes.—The four hereditary classes of society in India, each with its own occupation or profession, to be born in one of which is to remain in it, with no possibility of rising in the social world.

132. Casting Vote.—The vote by which a presiding officer decides a question when there is a tie vote (**807**).

133. Caucus.— (*a*) A preliminary meeting of members of the same political party to nominate candidates for local offices, to decide on party measures, to select delegates to conventions, etc. A primary (**638**).

(*b*) A secret meeting of legislators to nominate party candidates or to decide upon party measures.

134. Cavalry.—A body of soldiers mounted on horse back.

135. Caveat.—A descriptive notice of an invention intended to be patented, filed in the patent office before a formal application is made for a patent right (**581**).

2. It prevents the granting of a patent to another for the described invention during the life of the caveat.

3. It guarantees to the inventor time to mature his invention.

4. It must be limited to a single invention or improvement.

5. It operates for one year but may be renewed.

6. The fee is $10.

136. Census.—An official numbering of the whole people, together with the collecting of various general statistics.

2. The first United States census was taken in 1790, which showed an enumeration of 3,929,827. It was the first systematic census taken in the world.

3. The census is taken every ten years—every year ending with a cipher.

4. The census serves as a basis for appor-

tioning Representatives (**37**).

5. It is taken under the direction of the Interior Department (**324,7**).

6. A Superintendent of Census is appointed at \$5,000 per year, to supervise the taking of each particular census.

7. The whole country is divided into small census districts, and census enumerators are appointed to take the census in their respective districts at the same time.

137. Centralization.—The vesting of great power in the general government, as opposed to extensive local self-government.

2. Thus, France is divided into eighty-nine *departments*, all governed exactly alike, with headquarters at Paris. (*Bureaucracy*, **112**).

138. Certificates, Gold and Silver.—Bills or certificates issued by the government to those depositing gold or silver to the amount of five dollars or more, in the U. S. Treasury.

2. They pass as money, but are not legal tender, and are redeemable in the coin they call for, on demand.

139. Certiorari.—A writ issuing from a superior court to an inferior court, commanding the transfer to the former, of a cause pending in the latter; or demanding the record of a case adjusted in the lower court, to be reviewed by the superior court.

2. The writ may be issued on the application of either the plaintiff or the defendant.

3. Its object is the more certain and speedy justice to the aggrieved.

140. Challenging Votes.—The formal objecting, at the polls, to the permitting of particular persons to vote, on the ground that they are illegal voters.

2. A person challenged may not vote until the challenge is withdrawn or his right to vote is proven to the satisfaction of the election officers.

141. Charter.—A formal grant of certain rights, powers and privileges, duly executed in writing, made by the sovereign power of a state or country, to all the people or to a certain portion of them.

2. Also, a legislative act creating municipal or other corporations, setting forth their powers and privileges.

3. One of the colonial forms of government (**174**).

4. A charter differs from a constitution in that the former is *granted by a higher power,* while the latter is *established by the people.*

142. Chattel.—Personal property.

143. Check.—A written order on a bank for the immediate payment of money on deposit to the credit of the signer.

2. A *certified check* is one indorsed by the cashier as "*Good,*" for the payment of which the bank becomes responsible.

144. Chivalry.—(1000-1500). A military order composed of mounted, armed knights, pledged to the defense of the church and of the weak and oppressed in feudal times (**345**).

145. Circuit Court of Appeals, U. S.—The second grade of Federal Courts.

2. Congress established this court in 1891—

one in each of the nine Federal Circuits.

3. An additional Judge was appointed in each Circuit.

4. This court is held by a Justice of the Supreme Court and the two Circuit Judges. If either of these be absent, any District Judge within the circuit may act in his stead.

5. This court has *only appellate jurdictions*, hearing all cases appealed from the Circuit and District Courts, except those cases that by law are appealed directly to the Supreme Court.

6. Its officers are a Marshall and a Clerk, both of whom it appoints.

7. It has no juries.

8. Only certain important classes of cases may be appealed from this court to the Supreme Court.

146. Circuit Court, U. S.— The third grade of Federal Courts.

2. The entire Union, exclusive of the Territories, is divided into nine Judicial Federal Circuits.

3. Each Circuit comprises several States.

4. The Supreme Court assigns one of its nine Justices to each of the nine Federal Circuits, where he is required by law to hold court at least once in every two years.

5. Besides the Supreme Judge assigned to the circuit, the President appoints two Circuit Judges for each circuit.

6. The Circuit Court may be held by a Supreme Judge, a Circuit Judge, a District Judge, or any two of them, or all three to-

gether.

7. The Circuit Court has—

(1) Original jurisdiction in civil cases when the amount in controversy is $2,000 or more and an alien is a party or the suit is between citizens of different States: where the United States are petitioners, or any officer thereof is plaintiff.

(2) Original jurisdiction in cases under the copyright, patent, and revenue laws.

(3) Unlimited jurisdiction in Federal criminal cases, such as counterfeiting, etc.

(4) Exclusive jurisdiction in capital offenses against the United States.

8. Since the establishment of the Circuit Court of Appeals (145), the Circuit Court has no appellate jurisdiction (33).

9. It has a grand and a trial jury.

10. It holds two sessions a year in each State.

11. Each Circuit Judge appoints as many commissioners (184) in his circuit as he deems necessary.

12. The court officers are Judge, District Attorney (286.7). Marshal (501), and a Clerk who is appointed by the court.

147. Citizen.—"All persons born or naturalized in the United States, and subject to the jurisdiction thereof, are citizens of the United States and of the State wherein they reside."

2. Men, women, and children are citizens.

3. Chinese can not become naturalized.

4. Indians not taxed are not citizens. They may be made citizens (544,10).

5. A citizen is not necessarily a voter, but

all citizens have civil rights (**158**).

6. "The right of citizens of the United States to vote, shall not be denied or abridged by the United States, or by any State, on account of race, color, or previous condition of servitude."

7. *But a State may name any other qualification for voting.*

8. But if any male citizens, being 21 years of age, are denied the right to vote, by any State, except for rebellion or other crime, the number of Representatives of such State is reduced in the ratio that the number of such citizens bears to the whole number of male citizens 21 years of age in the State.

9. A person may be a citizen of the United States without being a citizen of a State—he may be a citizen of a Territory.

148. City, Town, Village.—A *city* is a limited territory very densely populated, exercising the right of local government, with special privileges under a charter from the State.

2. In some States, 1,000 inhabitants may obtain a city charter; in other States, 10,000; in Massachusetts, it requires 12,000.

3. A city is incorporated in order that it may provide for a fire department, water works, pavements, an organized police, etc.

4. In some States, the Legislature grants special charters; in others, cities are incorporated under general laws.

5. Every city has a mayor, a board of aldermen (**92**) or council, a treasurer, a clerk or recorder, a police force, a board of education,

a city attorney and other minor officers.

6. *Town* and *Village*, in most States, are synonymous terms meaning a smaller collection of dwellings than is required for a city, which town or village may, or may not, be incorporated; while a city is always incorporated.

7. In New England, the word *town* means the same as township or district in other States. (**163,2**).

149. Civics.—The science of civil government (**153**).

150. Civil.—From the Latin *civis*, meaning citizen; hence, pertaining to a citizen in his relations to other citizens or to the state.

151. Civil Action, or Suit.—An action brought to recover, enforce or protect a private right, or to prevent or redress a private wrong.

152. Civil Death.—The being deprived of civil rights and debarred from civil society by banishment, outlawry (**571**), etc.

153. Civil Government.—The power by which a state controls its citizens in their relations to each other and to the state.

154. Civil Law.—The law of the ancient Romans.

2. In Louisiana it takes the place of the common law (**189**), which prevails in all the other states, in cases not regulated by Statute law(**770**).

3. Civil law is sometimes used to denote the law governing civil suits, as opposed to criminal law.

155. Civil Liberty.—Freedom to do as one pleases, subject to law.

156. Civil Offense.—An offense against an individual or certain individuals, as distinguished from a crime, which is an offense against the public.

157. Civil Office.—Any office not military, created by Congress.

2. No Congressman may, during the time for which he is elected, hold such an office if it be created during such time, but he may do so after his term expires.

3. He may hold a military office thus created.

158.—Civil Right.—The right to enjoy a natural right (545) subject to law.

159. Civil Rights Bill.—An act passed by Congress April 9, 1866, over President Johnson's veto, making freedmen (365) citizens of the United States, violations under it to be considered by the Federal Courts alone.

2. It did not give them the right to vote. This right was conferred upon them later by the fifteenth Amendment to the Constitution.

160. Civil Service.—The whole body of officials appointed by the President and his subordinates, excepting the army and navy, to aid in carrying on the work of the government.

2. These number about 120,000.

161. Civil Service Commission.—A commission of three persons, not more than two of the same political faith, appointed by the President, with the consent of the Senate, to supervise examinations and to carry out the provisions of the Civil Service Act (162).

162. Civil Service Reform.—A system based

4

on the Civil Service Act of 1883, which makes ability as ascertained in competitive examinations, and not party politics as under the "Spoils System" (**752**), the test for appointment to certain inferior offices in the Civil Service (**161**).

2. The President is authorized to extend the civil service rule to offices not now included under it.

3. The act prohibits assessing Federal officers for political purposes, and it also prohibits Federal officers from engaging in active party service.

4. The President is not compelled to carry out the act.

163. Civil Unit or Civil District.—The district, or small political division in which the people exercise the minor judicial and executive functions of government directly.

2. In different States, the civil unit is known by different names; as the *Magisterial District*, of West Virginia and Virginia; the *Hundred*, of Delaware; the *Township*, of Ohio and many other States; the *Civil District*, of Tennessee, etc.

3. Each county comprises several civil units.

164. Civil War.—A war between sections or parties of the same country.

165. Clearance.—A certificate permitting a vessel to sail from port (**621**).

166. Clearing House.—An establishment where banks exchange their obligations and settle accounts between each other.

2. Every large city has a clearing house.

167. Club Law.—Government by violence or force; anarchy(29); lynch law (488).

168. Coast Trade.—The trade or commerce carried on between ports of the same country.

169. Cobden Club.—The great free-trade organization of England.

2. It derives its name from Richard Cobden, the great English free-trade champion.

170. Codicil.—A supplementary clause added to a will (852).

2. It must be executed with the same formality as the will itself.

171. Collector of Customs.—An officer appointed by the President to collect duties (296) on imported goods, at a customhouse (253).

172. Collusion.—A secret agreement between two or more persons to defraud some one.

173. Colonial Courts.—In the colonies, the system of courts, in general, was as follows, after the English plan:

1. The *Petty Sessions*, where a justice of the peace held court alone to try minor civil and criminal cases.

2. The *Quarter Sessions*, a court composed of all the justices of the peace of the county. It met quarterly to try cases appealed from the Petty Sessions.

3. The *Highest Court*, composed of the governor and his council, or of judges appointed by the governor.

174. Colonial Forms of Government.—The forms of government in the thirteen original colonies were as follows:

(1) *Royal* or *Provincial*—A government ad-

ministered by the king through a governor appointed by him.—New York, New Hampshire, Virginia, Georgia, New Jersey and the Carolinas.

(2) *Charter.*—A government in which the colonists governed under a charter from the king, granting them certain political rights and privileges.—Connecticut Massachusetts, and Rhode Island.

(3) *Proprietary.*—A government by a proprietor.—Pennsylvania, Maryland and Delaware.

2. In each case, the sovereignty of the Crown was maintained.

3. The Plymouth Colony acted independent of any power.

4. The London Company was a commercial corporation.

175. Colonization, P o l i t i c a l.—Fraudulently transferring voters from districts in which they are not needed, into doubtful districts, just before an election, in order that they may vote and thereby change the result of the election in the doubtful districts.

176. Colony.—A company of people living together in a foreign country and remaining subject to the government of the mother country.

177. Columbia.—A political name applied to the United States in honor of Columbus.

178. Comity of Nations.—The international courtesy by which one nation, within its territory or in its courts, recognizes, respects and makes effective the laws and peculiar institutions of another nation.

179. Commander-in-Chief.—The President is Commander-in-Chief of the army and navy of the United States, and of the State militia (514) when in the Federal service.

2. He may command in person, or he may, and usually does, appoint officers to command.

3. The Governor is Commander-in-Chief of the State miltia when not in the Federal service.

180. Commerce.—Trade; exchange of commodities.

2. A State can affect commerce only as follows:

(*1*) Commerce wholly within the State.

(*2*) By levying uniform duties with the consent of Congress (**201**).

(*3*) By inspection laws.

3. Congress regulates commerce with foreign nations, with the Indian tribes, and among the several States.

181. Commercial Law.—The rules and usages that regulate commercial transactions between merchants and traders generally.

2. It is derived from maritime and international law, and the customs of merchants.

182. Commercial Paper.—Negotiable paper given in the transaction of business, as notes, bank checks, etc.

183. Commission.—(*a*) A written certificate of appointment to office or position given by the proper authority.

(*b*) A person or persons appointed to perform certain duties; as the Electoral Commission (**302**).

184. Commissioner, U. S.—An officer whose

duty it is to cause the arrest of persons charged with crime against the United States, to hold them for trial, and to assist the United States Circuit and District Courts in taking evidence in Federal cases.

.2. The Circuit Court Judges appoint as many Commissioners in their respective circuits as they may deem necessary.

3. Congress provides by law, that any State or Federal Judge, or a magistrate, may perform the duties of Commissioner.

185. Commissary.—The army officer who provides food for the soldiers.

186. Commit.—(*a*) To imprison.

(*b*) To refer; as to refer a bill to a committee for examination and report.

187. Committee.—One or more persons elected or appointed from a body of men, to whom matters are referred for action or critical examination and report.

2. The first person named on a committee is usually the chairman.

3. The object in selecting committees is to dispatch business.

4. In legislative bodies, bills are almost invariably referred to committees before being considered by the houses.

5. The United States Senate *elects* its committees; in the House, the Speaker *appoints* them.

6. A *standing committee* is one that continues through a session or for a fixed time, for the consideration of matters of a definite class.

7. The United States Senate has about thirty standing committees; the House of Representatives, over fifty.

8. A *special* or *select* *committee* is one selected to do a certain thing, or to consider a special question.

9. A *committee of the whole* consists of all the members of a legislative or deliberative body resolved, on the motion of a member, into one general committee, for the full consideration and free debate of a special subject.

(*1*) When a body resolves itself into a committee of the whole, the presiding officer vacates the chair and names some member of the body to occupy it.

(*2*) A committee of the whole can not take final action in a matter; neither can it adjourn. When its deliberations are complete, some member moves that the committee "*now rise;*" the regular presiding officer then resumes the chair, and the chairman of the committee "reports progress" or "recommendations," after which alone, is a motion to adjourn in order.

10. A *conference committee* is (*a*) a committee appointed by one body to confer with a like committee from another body on questions of difference between them, with a view to arrive at some agreement; or

(*b*) These two committees organized as one. (*Political Committees* 608).

188. Common Council.—The legislative body, or the lower branch of the same, of a city or other municipal corporation.

189. Common Law.—The unwritten law, based on long established custom, or precedents established by former decisions of courts of justice.

2. It is applied by courts in England and in all the States, except Louisiana—where the Civil Law (154) takes its place—to all cases not regulated by statute law, to which it gives way in every instance.

190. Commonwealth.—A state. A free or popular government. Not an absolute government.

191. Communism.—The theory of distributing all wealth equally among men; or of common ownership and use of all wealth.

192. Commutation.—The substitution of a milder punishment for one more severe.

193. Compact.—A solemn agreement or contract.

2. In the Constitution, a temporary agreement.

3. No State can enter into a compact with another State or foreign power without the consent of Congress.

194. Complaint.—A formal allegation or accusation against a person, made or directed to a proper court or officer, for the purpose of instituting a suit.

195. Compromise.—A settlement of matters of dispute between parties by mutual concessions.

196. Comptroller.—A public officer who examines, adjusts and certifies accounts.

197. Concurrent Resolution.—A resolution

agreed to by both houses of an assembly but
not intended to have the force of law.

198. Confederacy, Confederation.—A league
or compact between two or more independent allied States or nations, as opposed to a
union of the people.

2. States are prohibited from entering into
any confederation or alliance.

199. Confederate States of America.—T h e
government organized Feb. 4, 1861, by the seceded States at the beginning of the Civil War,
with Jefferson Davis as President, and Alexander H. Stephens. Vice-President.

200. Confiscation.—The forfeiting of property, and the appropriation of it, by the government, to public use.

201. Congress.—The supreme law-making
body of the United States. It consists of the
Senate, or the upper house (**724**), and the
House of Representatives, or the lower house
(**399**).

2. It meets at Washington regularly once a
year, on the first Monday in December.

3. It may, by law, appoint a day to meet,
other than the first Monday in December. It
has done so at different times, but it always returned to the day named.

4. It may be called in extra session by the
President at any time,—either one or both
houses.

5. Members of each house (except the Speaker of the House, who receives $8,000 per year)
receive the same salary —$5,000 per year.

6. Members have been paid different sala-

ries as follows: 1789 to 1815, $6.00 per day; 1815 to 1817, $1,500 per year; 1817 to 1855, $8.00 per day; 1855 to 1865, $3,000 per year; 1865 to 1871, $5,000 per year; 1871 to 1874, $7,500 per year; 1874 to the present time, $5,000 per year.

7. The salaries of all members have always been the same, except in 1795, when Senators received $7.00 per day, and Representatives received $6.00 per day.

8. In addition to his salary, each member is allowed 20 cents per mile traveled in going to, and returning from each session of Congress.

9. Each member has a private secretary at $1,200 per year, paid by the government.

10. The salary of members is fixed by law of Congress, and is paid out of the National Treasury.

11. After each census (since 1850) Congress decides the number of members the House of Representatives shall have during the ensuing ten years, beginning the third year after the census is taken. This number may be increased by the admission of new States.

12. "*A Congress*" means the two branches holding office during one representative term of two years. Thus, a new Congress comes into power every two years, when new Representatives are elected, they all being elected every even year, though the Senate is a perpetual body, being at no time made up wholly of new members.

13. The different Congresses are designated

by ordinal number. For example, the LVIth Congress came into power March 4th, 1899, and the LVIIth Congress will come into power March 4th, 1900.

14. Members can not be arrested while attending, nor while going to, or returning from, Congress, except for treason, felony, or breach of the peace.

15. For any speech or debate in Congress, members shall not be questioned in any other place.

16. By a two-thirds of a quorum vote of each house taken by yeas and nays, Congress can pass a bill, order, resolution or vote over the veto of the President.

17. Every bill, order, resolution or vote having the effect of law, must be presented to the President for his approval before the same shall take effect.

18. The President may adjourn Congress when the two houses can not agree as to the time of adjournment; but this has never yet been done.

19. Congress may, and does, make regulations governing the election of Senators and Representatives, "*except as to the place of choosing Senators*," but it may grant the privilege to the State Legislatures.

20. Each house is judge of the elections, returns, and qualifications of its own members.

21. A majority of each house constitutes a quorum to transact business; but a smaller number may (*a*) adjourn from day to day, and (*b*) compel the attendance of absent

members under penalty.

22. Each house may punish its members for disorderly conduct in any way it deems proper, and may expel members by a two-thirds vote.

23. By a decision of the Supreme Court, Congress and Legislatures may punish persons not members for cause; but only by imprisonment, and then not beyond the dissolution of the house inflicting the punishment.

24. Each house must keep and publish a journal of its proceedings, except such parts as require secrecy.

25. The *Congressional Record* is a daily paper printed by Congress, containing the full proceedings of the previous day, including speeches of members, many of which were never delivered in either house, but are printed as a matter of record.

26. A yea and nay vote must be taken on any question in either house, if one-fifth of the members present demand it.

27. All sessions of Congress are open to the public, except the executive sessions of the Senate (726,6).

28. "No Senator or Representative shall, during the time for which he was elected, be appointed to any civil office under the authority of the United States which shall have been created, or the emoluments whereof shall have been increased, during such time," but he may be so appointed after his term has expired.

29. No person can hold another Federal office and be a member of Congress at the

same time.

30. A person may hold a State office and at the same time be a member of Congress unless prohibited by his State constitution.

31. Resolutions proposing amendments to the Constitution, or to adjourn, do not require the approval of the President.

32. No member of Congress or other Federal officer may act as a Presidential Elector.

33. All members are sworn to support the Constitution, etc., before entering upon the duties of office.

34. No person once a Federal or State officer sworn to support the Constitution, etc., and who afterwards engaged in rebellion or insurrection, or aided the enemies of the government, can become a member of Congress or hold any other Federal or State office.   But Congress, by a two-thirds vote of each house, may remove the disability.

(*U. S. Senators*, **725;** *Representatives*, **686.**)

202. Congressional District.—One of the divisions into which a State Legislature divides the State for the purpose of electing United States Representatives (**686**).

2. Each District elects one Representative.

3. The Districts must be contiguous.

4. They are numbered first, second, etc.

5. A State is re-districted whenever its representation in Congress changes.

203. Congressman.—A United States Senator or Representative.

2. But the term is ordinarily applied to Representatives only.

204. Congressman-at-Large.—A Representative elected on the general State ticket.

2. After any census, when a State receives an increased number of Representatives, and the Legislature fails to re-district the State before the next congressional election, the additional member or members are elected on the general State ticket.

3. By the census of 1880, Maine's representation was decreased, and in 1882, Congress permitted all her Representatives to be elected on the general State ticket.

205. Connecticut Constitution.—The first written constitution recorded in history; known as the *"Fundamental Orders of Connecticut."*

2. It was framed in 1639, and continued in force until 1818.

3. It did not mention the king, and gave every citizen the right to vote.

206. Connivance.—The guilty sanctioning of wrong-doing by pretending ignorance of it, and thus failing to prevent it, although it is possible to do so.

207. Conscription or Draft.—A compulsory enlisting of men in the army and navy.

2. Congress has power to authorize drafts.

3. The power was exercised in the Civil War.

208. Conservatives.—Those opposed to any change in existing institutions and established forms of government.

209. Consignee.—A person to whom another sends goods to be sold on commission.

210. Consignment.—A bill of goods sent by one person to another to be sold for the consignor.

211. Consignor.—A person who sends goods to another person to be sold on commission.

212. Conspiracy.—A secret combination of two or more men to do some unlawful act; as to commit treason, etc.

213. Conspirator.—One who takes part in a conspiracy.

214. Constable.—A ministerial officer of a justice's court. He serves legal papers, makes arrests, preserves the peace, etc.

2. His term of office and jurisdiction are the same as those of the justice.

215. Constituent.—One who is represented by another in a legislative assembly.

(*b*) One for whom another acts.

216. Constitution.—The fundamental law of a country, which takes precedence over all other law, and with which all other laws of the country must agree.

2. The Constitution of the United States and of Great Britain differ in that the former is a written constitution, while the latter is unwritten.

217. Constitution, Federal.—The fundamental law of the United States, in harmony with which all other laws must be made.

2. The history of the Constitution is as follows:

(*1*) In 1785, Virginia and Maryland disagreed about the navigation and fisheries of the Potomac River and Chesapeake Bay. They appointed commissioners to settle the dispute. These commissioners met and decided that the question involved the rights of other States. They recommended a convention of all the States to consider the question, and then adjourned. Thus,

(*2*) The *Annapolis* (Maryland) *Convention* met in 1786. But only five States were represented. Owing to the smallness of the representation and the importance of the question, this convention adjourned after simply recommending to Congress and the States, the calling of another general convention. This was done, and,

(*3*) The *Constitutional Convention* met at Philadelphia in May, 1787, "For the sole and exclusive purpose of revising the Articles of Confederation." They soon found this a hopeless task, and set to work to draft a new Constitution, which they completed after almost four months of hard ork.

3. All the States except Rhode Island were represented in this convention.

4. The work of the Constitutional Couvention threatened to be a failure because of disagreements on the questions of (*a*) *taxation*, (*b*) *the powers to be given the general government*, and (*c*) *State representation in Congress;* especially the latter point. These differences were finally compromised.

5. The *"Connecticut Compromise"* settled the great question of representation in Congress. The larger States wanted representation according to population, while the smaller States held for equal State representation.

6. Connecticut, as it happened, had a Legis-

lature peculiar to itself. It elected its upper house on the general State ticket, while the members of the lower house represented townships; therefore, Connecticut proposed that Congress be composed of two houses, the Senate to represent the States, with an equal representation from each State regardless of its size, and the House of Representatives to represent the people according to the population of the States. This proposition was adopted, giving us the famous "Connecticut Compromise" of history.

7. The ratification of *nine* States made the Constitution binding between those States.

8. Having been ratified by *eleven* States, the Constitution went into effect March 4th, 1789.

9. *North Carolina* (November 21st, 1789) and *Rhode Island* (May 29th, 1790) ratified the Constitution *after it went into effect.*

10. The Constitution derives its authority from the people.

11. The purposes of the Constitution are:

(*1*) To form a more perfect union.

(*2*) To establish justice.

(*3*) To insure domestic tranquillity.

(*4*) To provide for the common defense.

(*5*) To promote the general welfare.

(*6*) To secure the blessings of liberty.

12. *Amendments to the Constitution* may be proposed in two ways;

(*1*) By Congress, two-thirds of both houses agreeing thereto; or (*2*) on the application of the Legislatures of two-thirds of the States, Congress *shall* call a convention to propose

5

amendments.

13. Amendments may be ratified in either of two ways:

(*1*) By the Legislatures of three-fourths of the States, or

(*2*) By conventions in three-fourths thereof, as Congress may direct.

14. No conventions have ever been called either to propose or to ratify amendments.

15. In all, *nineteen* amendments have been proposed, of which *fifteen* have been ratified, and *four* have been rejected.

16. The first Congress proposed twelve amendments, ten of which, constituting our American Bill of Rights (84), were adopted.

17. An amendment proposed or ratified, does not require the approval of the President.

18. The Constitution may be amended in any respect, *except* to deprive a State, without its consent, of equal suffrage in the Senate.

19. The Constitution consists of *seven* Articles and *fifteen* Amendments.

218. Consul—An officer appointed by the President, with the consent of the Senate, to represent the commercial interests of the government in foreign countries.

2. His principal duties are:

(*1*) To care for the commercial interests of our country— his most important duty.

(*2*) To protect our citizens abroad, and our seamen.

(*3*) To care for destitute seamen at the expense of the United States.

(*4*) To cause mutinous seamen to be arrested and sent home for trial.

(*5*) To hold the papers of American vessels while in port, and to keep a record of such vessels as to tonnage, cargoes, seamen, etc.

(*6*) To care for, and to deliver to, the national treasury to be held for the legal heirs, property of American citizens dying abroad.

(*7*) To hold consular courts (**219**).

(*8*) To collect commercial, manufacturing and agricultural statistics of the country wherein he resides.

(*6*) To execute for Americans abroad, legal documents to be used in this country.

3. A *Consul General* is a consul of the highest rank; he has jurisdiction over several consuls or in several different places.

4. There are over three hundred consuls, and about thirty consuls-general.

5. Some consuls-general are ministers resident (**283,9**).

6. A *Vice Consul* is a person appointed to act in the place of a consul during his absence or in case of his removal.

7. The foreign countries with whom we deal are divided into consular districts, in the principal cities of which the consuls reside.

8. Consuls receive from $1,000 to $6,000 each per year.

9. Some consuls are paid by fees.

10. Consuls are subject to the laws of the countries in which they reside, while ministers are not.

11. Consuls who receive small salaries, or who are paid by fees, may engage in business on their own account. Others must not do so.

12. The duties of consuls are commercial; not political.

13. Consuls deal with individuals rather than with governments. Ministers deal with governments.

219. Consular Court.—A court held in a foreign country, by a Consul, to settle disputes between seamen, and between Americans and foreigners in regard to commercial matters; in some countries it tries cases between the countries and American citizens; as in China, Japan, Turkey and Siam.

220. Consular Service.—The consular service consists of the whole body of consuls (**218**) or commercial agents of the government, residing at the principal seaports of foreign countries.

221. Contempt.—(*a*) Wilful and disrespectful disobedience to the orders, rules and processes of a legislative assembly or of a court.

(*b*) Insolent or contemptuous language or behavior in the presence of a court.

2. Legislative bodies and courts are empowered to punish contempt (**201**, 23).

222. Continental Congress.—The body of representatives of the thirteen colonies that met from 1774 to 1781.

2. A Continental Congress was first proposed by Benjamin Franklin.

3. The *First Continental Congress* met at Philadelphia September 5th, 1774,

to discuss the common interests of the colonies. It set forth a declaration of the rights and wrongs of the colonies, and passed resolutions and made recommendations pointing to the Revolution.

4. The *Second Continental Congress* met at Philadelphia May 10th, 1775, and later at six other different places. It held its last session October, 1788; but, theoretically, it was in perpetual session from 1775 until March, 1781, when the Articles of Confederation (52) went into effect. It was the governing power during the revolutionary period.

223. Contested Elections in Congress.—1. *In the House:* (1) The defeated candidate must serve notice of contest on his opponent, with the grounds of contest, within thirty days after the returns have been declared.

(2) Within the next thirty days, the successful candidate must serve an answer on the contestant, stating the grounds of his defense.

(3) Forty days are allowed the contestant, and forty to the member-elect for taking testimony before a proper officer; and ten days more are allowed to the contestant for taking testimony in rebuttal.

(4) The testimony is mailed to the Clerk of the House, and is referred to the committee on elections.

(5) The committee reports, and the House decides the contest by a majority vote.

(6) The contestant is usually allowed not over $2,000 for expenses.

2. *In the Senate:* (*1*) The question goes directly to the Committee on Elections; a report is made, and the Senate decides by a majority vote.

(*2*) In all contests, the member-elect serves till the contest is decided.

224. Contraband Goods.—Articles particularly useful in carrying on war, which, by international law, neutrals are prohibited from supplying to an enemy.

2. Such goods may be seized, condemned in a prize court (**642**), and confiscated (**200**) to the captors.

3. During the Civil War, negro slaves were contraband of war.

225. Contract.—An agreement between two or more persons to do, or not to do, a certain thing or things.

2. A *verbal contract* is one not reduced to writing.

3. A *written contract* is one that is reduced to writing, and signed by the parties.

4. A *parol contract* is either a verbal or written contract not under seal nor recorded.

5. A contract not to be performed within a year must be reduced to writing, to make it binding.

6. To make a contract binding, there must be a sufficient consideration therefor.

7. The Constitution forbids States from passing laws impairing the obligations of contracts.

226. Conveyance.—A written instrument by which the title to property is transferred from one person to another.

227. Convict —A person convicted of crime and sentenced to penal servitude.

228. Copyright.—The exclusive right of an author, inventor, or proprietor to print, reprint, publish and sell his own literary or artistic productions.

2. The power to regulate copyrights is vested in Congress.

3. States can not grant copyrights; they did so prior to the adoption of the Constitution in 1789.

4. A copyright is granted for a term of 28 years and can be renewed for 14 years upon application made within six months before the expiration of the first term.

5. The following may be copyrighted: A book, map, chart, dramatic or musical composition, engraving, cut, print, or photograph or negative thereof, or of a painting, drawing, chromo, statue, statuary, and of models or designs intended to be perfected as works of the fine arts.

6. A copyright is assignable, but the assignment must be recorded in the office of the Librarian of Congress within sixty days from its date.

7. The fee for assignment is $1.00, and for each copy thereof, $1.00.

8. The fee for a copyright is fifty cents, and for each certificate under seal, of such copyright, fifty cents.

9. To obtain a copyright, a printed or typewritten copy of the title of the book, map,

etc., or a description of the statue or painting, etc., must be sent to the Librarian of
Congress at Washington D. C.; and not later
than the day of publication, two copies of the
best edition of the book or publication, or a
photograph of the statue or other article,
must be sent to the Librarian, and a copy of
every subsequent edition containing substan-
tial changes must also be sent.

10. Every copy of a book or other thing
copyrighted, must bear the words; " Copyright, 18— , by— , " or, " Entered according
to act of Congress, in the year -- , by-- , in
the office of the Librarian of Congress at
Washington."

11. The inscription is placed on the title page
or on the page next following, in the book,
or upon some visible portion of the article
copyrighted.

12. A penalty of $100.00 is imposed on any
person using the copyright notice on any book
or article not copyrighted.

13. A foreigner, whose nation grants the
same privilege to American citizens, may copyright his productions in this country, but
books thus copyrighted must be printed in
the United States.

14. The fee for a copyright in this country
in the case of a foreigner is $1.00 with an ad-
ditional fee of fifty cents for each certificate of
entry desired.

15. The United States has international
copyright (429) treaties with Belgium, France,
Great Britain, Switzerland, Germany, Italy,

Portugal and Spain.

16. *Trade Marks* and *Labels* are not copyrighted, but are registered in the Patent Office, the registry fee being $25.00 and $6.00 respectively.

17. Full information on the subject of copyrights may be obtained by addressing the Librarian of Cogress, Washington D. C.

229. Copperhead. —A northern sympathizer with the South during the Civil War.

230. Coroner. —A county officer whose duty it is to inquire into the suspicious, mysterious, or violent death of persons, or into death occurring in prison.

2. When notified of such death, the coroner summons a jury which varies in number from 6 to 15, examines witnesses, and a written verdict is rendered.

3. The judicial inquiry of a coroner is called a *coroner's inquest* (**424**).

231. Coroner's Jury.—A jury summoned by a coroner to determine the cause of, or the responsibility for, a mysterious, violent or sudden death, or death in prison.

232. Corporation.—A body of persons chartered under the law, to act as one person (**141,2**), and capable of perpetuating its existence by the addition of new members.

2. A *public corporation* is a municipal organization; as a city or town, possessing certain privileges of local government.

3. A *private corporation* is a corporate body of private individuals engaged in any business or enterprise on their own account.

4. A corporation may sue and be sued as a single individual.

5. The individual members of a corporation are not personally responsible for its acts, except where made so by special statute.

6. A corporation may be dissolved:

(*1*) By the death of all its members.

(*2*) By the surrender of its charter.

(*3*) By the forfeiture of its charter.

(*4*) By legislative act.

233. Corruption of Blood.—The disability of a person to inherit or transmit property on account of being convicted of treason.

2. It is forbidden by the Constitution.

234. Counterfeiting.—Making or knowingly passing false coin, bonds, notes, revenue or postage stamps, or any other securities of the government.

2. The Constitution gives Congress power to pass laws to punish counterfeiting, which it has done by fine and imprisonment, according to circumstances.

3. The penalty for making or passing counterfeit coin is a fine not exceeding $5,000 and imprisonment not exceeding ten years. When notes are counterfeited, the term of imprisonment may be fifteen years.

4. Counterfeiting the money, bonds, etc., of a foreign government, within the United States, is punishable by a fine not exceeding $5,000, and imprisonment not exceeding five years.

5. States may also punish counterfeiting.

235. Countersign.—A private military

watchword or signal, used to prevent unauthorized persons from passing a line of sentries, who are ordered to allow none to pass who can not give it.

2. The commanding officer changes it every day.

236. County.—A political division next smaller than a State.

2. It has its own officers differing in the different States and it administers its own local affairs.

3. Every State is thus divided; these divisions, in Louisiana, are called parishes.

237. Coupon.—A certificate, attached to bonds, representing interest, to be detached and presented for payment when due.

238. Court.—A tribunal legally established for the trying of cases and the administering of justice.

239. Court in Banc, or Banco.—A full sitting of a superior law court at regular sessions when every member is present and occupies his respective place, to hear arguments of questions of *law*, as distinguished from sittings at *nisi prius*, (551) where, generally, a single individual presides, and *civil suits* are tried by jury.

240. Court Martial.—A court composed of military or naval officers, which tries all violations of military and naval laws.

241. Court of Claims.—A court established by Congress to hear and determine all disputed claims against the United States.

2. It consists of one Chief Justice and four

Associate Justices, appointed by the President with the consent of the Senate. These hold office during good behavior, and receive $4,500 each per year.

3. It is in session at Washington almost the whole year.

4. It reports regularly to Congress, which body generally provides for claims favorably reported. It can only *recommend* the payment of claims.

5. The fact that the government can not be sued, makes this court necessary. Before the establishment of this court, claims could only be secured by petitioning Congress.

242. Court of Impeachment.—The United States Senate or a State Senate, sitting as a tribunal to try impeachments (404).

243. Court of Record.—A court whose acts and judicial proceedings are all recorded and preserved for future reference.

244. Covenant.—A solemn contract or agreement under seal.

245. "Cradle of American Liberty."—Faneuil Hall, Boston, where the sturdy revolutionary patriots were wont to assemble to discuss the question of American independence.

246. Credentials.—Authentic written evidence that a person has the right to exercise official power; as certficates of election, the letters given by a government to ambassadors, consuls, etc.

247. Crime.—An offense against the public; a violation of law whereby the offender becomes accountable to the public and liable to punishment by the commonwealth, as distinguished from a private wrong or civil injury, for which he is accountable only to the individual injured. Crimes are divided into felonies (**344**) and misdemeanors (**523**).

248. Criminal Action, or Suit.—An action brought to convict and punish a criminal. In a criminal action, the United States or the State is always plaintiff.

249. Criminal Law.—The law that defines the nature and punishment of crimes (**247**).

250. Cross-Examination.—The examination of a witness by the party not calling him.

2. Leading questions (**465**) may be asked the witness in cross-examination, but not in direct examination(**284**).

251. Cumulative Vote.—A system which gives to each voter as many votes as there are candidates for a given office and allows him to cast them all for one candidate or to distribute them among the candidates as he chooses (**119**).

252. Currency.—(*a*) The money of a country, either paper or coin. (*b*) Commonly, paper money.

253. Custom-house.—The building where customs or duties are collected, and where vessels are entered (**316**) or cleared (**165**).

2. Custom-houses are established, one in each district, at different points along the seacoast, or navigable rivers, and on the boundary lines between the United States, Canada and Mexico.

3 The largest custom-house in the world is

at New Orleans.

4. It was over thirty years in completing; it contains 111 rooms, and cost $4,900,000.

254. Dark Horse.—A person whose name is unexpectedly, and at a late hour, presented to a nominating convention as a candidate.

255. Days of Grace.—The three days allowed by banks for the payment of a note or a draft after it becomes due.

256. Death Warrant.—An order signed by the proper authority for the execution of a criminal.

257. Deathwatch.—The guard placed over a criminal sentenced to death.

258. Deadlock.—The condition of being unable to transact business in Congress or other body on account of the members being so divided on political or other questions that the required majority can not be secured.

259. Debenture.—(*a*) A written acknowledgment of a debt.

(*b*) A certificate given at a custom-house entitling an exporter of imported goods to a drawback of duties paid on the same when they were imported.

260. Declaration of Independence.— The Declaration adopted by the Continental Congress July 4th, 1776, in which the Thirteen American Colonies formally declared themselves free and independent States, subject in no way to the government of Great Britain.

2. On June 7th, 1776, Richard Henry Lee of Virginia proposed a resolution in Congress, declaring the Colonies free and independent

States, and a committee consisting of Thomas Jefferson, John Adams, Benjamin Franklin, Roger Sherman and Robert R. Livingston, was appointed to draft a formal declaration, which was adopted. July 4th, 1776.

3. The document is a master piece of English and is now preserved in Washington.

4. When President John Hancock signed the declaration, he remarked; "We must be unanimous; there must be no pulling different ways; we must all hang together," to which Benjamin Franklin replied; "Yes, we must all hang together, or we shall all hang separately."

261. Declaration of Rights.—The declaration framed by the Stamp Act Congress (**758**) in 1765.

2. A similar declaration protesting against the more recent oppressive acts of Parliament, was issued by the First Continental Congress (**222,3**) in 1774.

3. Another similar declaration was embodied in the Declaration of Independence (**260**).

262. Declaratory Act.—An act of Parliament March 7, 1766, accompanying the repeal of the Stamp Act(**757**), vindicating Parliament in its previous harsh treatment of the Colonies, and declaring that it had the right to exercise power over them in any way whatsoever.

263. Deed.—A written instrument under seal acknowledged before a proper officer, and delivered, by which the title to real estate is transferred from one person to another.

2. A *warranty deed* is one in which the grantor or maker covenants to warrant and defend the title to the property conveyed against all claims whatsoever.

3. A *quit claim deed* is one in which the grantor releases simply the interest he has in the property.

4. A *trust deed* or *deed of trust,* is a deed by which property is conveyed to a third person as security for the payment of a debt to a second person on the payment of which it becomes void.

5. All deeds, to be valid, must be recorded.

264. Defalcation.—Embezzlement (**309**).

265. Defaulter.—A person who fails to account for money entrusted to his care; especially public money.

266. Defendant.—One against whom a civil or criminal action is brought.

267. Delegate.—(*a*) A person elected by the people of a Territory, to represent them in the House of Representatives (**399**). He may debate and serve on committees and make motions, but he can not vote. His term of office is two years. His compensation is the same as that of a Representative.

(*b*) A person selected by his constituents to represent them in a convention.

268. Delegates-at-Large.—The four delegates selected from each State without regard to congressional districts, to represent the United States Senators of the given State in the National Convention(**609**, 14).

269. Delegate Convention.—A convention composed of delegates (267) selected by their party or by the people to represent them.

270. Demagogue.—A politician who seeks to gain influence by flattery and deceit, and by working on the ignorance of the people.

271. Demonetization.—The withdrawing any kind of money from current use as a legal tender; as the demonetization of the silver dollar in 1873.

272. Demurrer.—A declaration of a defendant that, admitting the facts alleged by the plaintiff, yet they constitute no cause of action against the former, and that he will proceed no further in the case until the court has passed on the question.

273. Denizen.—A person not a native, who has been given all or certain rights of citizenship.

274. Deponent.—One who makes a deposition or gives written testimony under oath.

275. Deposit Fund, U. S.—A surplus fund of about $30,000,000 that the national government, in 1836, deposited with the several States then existing, to be kept by them until called for by Congress.

2. It has never been called in, and very probably never will be.

3. The States generally use it for school purposes.

276. Deposition.—The testimony of a witness under oath, reduced to writing by a competent officer before whom it is given, to be used in a given case in a court of justice.

2. The opposing party must be notified of the time and place of taking the deposition, in order that he may be present to cross-examine (**250**) the witness.

277. Despot.—An absolute monarch; the tyrannical ruler of an absolute-monarchy.

278. Despotism.—An absolute monarchy ruled by a tyrant.

279. Dilatory Motion.—(*a*) A motion made by a defendant in order to break down or delay an action against him without entering into a trial upon the merits of the case; as a motion to quash (**661**).

(*b*) Any motion made in any assembly for the purpose of hindering business.

280. Dilatory Plea.—A plea made for the sole purpose of causing delay in the trial of a case.

281. Diplomacy.—The art of conducting and adjusting the relations between states or nations.

282. Diplomat or Diplomatist.—One skilled or engaged in diplomacy (**281**).

283. Diplomatic Service.—The diplomatic service consists of the whole body of agents sent to foreign nations to represent our government in a *political* capacity.

2. These agents are appointed by the President, with the consent of the Senate.

3. They reside at the capitals of the countries to which they are accredited.

4. They represent the dignity of the government, and act in a political capacity alone.

5. They act under the direction of the Presi-

dent as he instructs them through the Secretary of State.

6. All messages to other countries are sent to them to be delivered, and all messages from other countries are received through them.

7. Their duties are to negotiate treaties, to protect the persons and property of United States citizens abroad, to furnish information to our government, and, in general, to act for our government in all diplomatic matters.

8. The powers and duties of all diplomatic agents are about the same. In general, these agents differ only in rank, dignity and salary.

9. There are four grades of diplomatic agents, as follows, beginning with the highest:

(1) Ambassadors.

(2) Envoys Extraordinary and Ministers Plenipotentiary.

(3) Ministers Resident.

(4) Charges D'Affaires.

10. By the law of nations, diplomatic agents, their families, secretaries and servants, are not subject to the laws of the countries wherein they reside. They can not be arrested, imprisoned or prosecuted. But if they conduct themselves improperly, they may be sent home.

11. Ambassadors receive from $12,000 to $17,500 per year. The other grades of diplomatic agents receive from $5,000 to $17,500.

12. We send ambassadors to Great Britain, France, Germany and Italy.

13. An ambassador or minister *in ordinary*, lives in the country to which he is accredited, and is intrusted with the ordinary business of a foreign minister.

14. An ambassador or envoy *extraordinary* is sent to a foreign country on a particular mission, and returns when the special business on which he is sent is accomplished.

15. A minister or envoy *plenipotentiary* has full power to act in all matters according to his own judgment, without referring them back to his government for instructions.

16. Secretaries of Legation (**718**) are appointed by the President to accompany diplomatic agents as their secretaries.

284. Direct Examination, or Examination in Chief.—The examination of a witness by the party calling him.

2. In direct examination, leading questions (**495**) are not permitted.

285. Disfranchise.—To deprive of a franchise (**359**); as of the right to hold office, etc.

286. District Court, U. S.—The lowest grade of Federal Courts.

2. The nine Judicial Circuits are divided into over sixty Judicial Districts, in each of which a resident District Judge is appointed by the President, and a District Court is established.

3. Each State comprises from one to three Districts. These Districts never cross State lines.

4. When necessary, a Circuit Judge may preside over a District Court, or one District Judge may hold court for another.

5. This court has original Jurisdiction only. It may try any crime committed within the District against the United States, except offenses punishable by death, which the Circuit Court alone can try. It can try certain civil cases under the Federal laws, when the amount involved exceeds $50.00; and it has exclusive original jurisdiction in all admiralty and maritime cases (15).

6. All cases may be appealed from the District Courts to the Circuit Court of Appeals.

7. A *District Attorney*, who represents the United States in all Federal cases in his District, in both Circuit and District Courts, and a *United States Marshal*, who is the sheriff of the Circuit and District Courts, are appointed by the President with the consent of the Senate, for each Federal District, to serve four years.

8. This Court has a grand and a trial jury.

9. It holds four sessions each year.

287. Divine Right of Kings.—The theory that kings have a divine right to rule, regardless of the people; that their authority to rule is direct from God, to whom alone they are responsible.

288. Division of the House.—A standing vote demanded when a *viva voce* vote (837) is close and doubtful and one side thinks the presiding officer is likely to decide against it.

2. The phrase originated in the English Parliament, where opposing sides march out on opposite sides of the hall to be counted.

289. Dixie.—A term applied to the Southern

States collectively.

290. Domain—The whole territory governed by a state or nation, with everything in it.

2. The *public domain* is the public lands, or the territory belonging to, and under the exclusive control of, a nation or a state; as the public lands in the West.

3. *Eminent domain* is the right of a state to take private property (only real estate) for public use, when necessary, by paying a fair value for it.

291. Double Standard.—The concurrent use of gold and silver as standards of money value.

292. Dower.—The share of a husband's property that legally goes to his wife at his death; usually one-third.

293. Draft.—(*a*) A conscription (**207**). (*b*) A bill of exchange. (*c*)An order from one party to a second party, directing the payment of money to a third. (*d*) A *sight draft* is payable as soon as presented and accepted (**1**), allowing days of grace (**255**). (*e*) A *time draft* is payable at the time shown on its face—so many days after sight, or presentation and acceptance, plus the days of grace. (*f*) An *accepted draft* (**1**) is negotiable. (*g*) A draft is not binding until accepted(**1**).

294. Duel.—A fight between two persons, by mutual agreement, with deadly weapons. Most States now expressly forbid dueling.

295. Duress.—The restraint of one's liberty by unlawful imprisonment, or by threatened violence to himself or to his near relatives, to such a degree as to influence his actions against his will.

296. Duties or Customs.—Taxes levied on imports (**407**) and exports (**332**).

2. The Constitution prohibits the taxation of exports; hence in the United States, duties apply exclusively to taxes on imports.

3. "All duties, imposts (**408**) and excises (**321**), shall be uniform throughout the United States."—*Constitution.*

4. All duties must be paid in gold by the importer (**296,4**), to the collectors of customs (**171**), at the custom-houses (**253**).

5. Duties are of two kinds; *specific* and *ad valorem.*

6. *Specific duty* is a tax on goods according to quantity or weight.

7. *Ad valorem duty* is a tax on the invoice or cost price of the goods in the country from which they come.

8. When ad valorem duties are to be paid, the importer must swear to the invoice price of the goods. If he swears falsely, the goods are confiscated(**200**) to the government, and he may be punished otherwise.

9. Congress alone can levy duties, except that a State may lay such duties as are absolutely necessary for executing its inspection laws, in the matters of expenses, and these laws must be subject to the revision and control of Congress, and all above sufficient to pay such expenses, if any, must go to the United States treasury.

10. Under the Articles of Confederation (**54**)

the States levied duties independent of each other.

297. Elastic Clause.—Article 1, Section viii, Clause 18, of the Constitution, which gives Congress power "to make all laws which shall be necessary and proper for carrying into execution the foregoing powers and all other powers vested by this Constitution in the government of the United States or in any department or office thereof."

2. Hamilton held that the clause should be construed liberally, while Jefferson held that it should be construed strictly.

3. Thus originated, in 1789, American political parties, under the names of "loose-constructionists," or Federal party (**339**), and "strict-constructionists," or Anti-Federal party, with Hamilton and Jefferson as leaders respectively.

298. Elect.—(*a*) To choose for office. (*b*) One chosen to an office which he has not yet assumed; as President-elect.

299. Elective Franchise.—The right to vote for public officers.

300. Elective Office.—An office to be filled by election.

301 Elector.—(*a*) Any legal voter. (*b*) A member of the Electoral College (**302**).

302. Electoral College.—The whole body of electors chosen by the voters of the United States to elect a President and Vice-President.

2 There are 447 electors, or as many as there are United States Senators and Representatives.

3. Necessary to a choice, 224.

4. State Legislatures provide for the manner of choosing electors.

5. They are now, in all the States, nominated in State Conventions and elected by law on the first Tuesday following the first Monday in November every four years—leap years, regularly.

6. Vacancies in the Electoral College are filled according to the laws of the State in which the vacancies occur; usually by the other electors.

7. Electors meet by law in their respective States on the *Second Monday in January* following their election.

8. Each State Legislature designates a place of meeting—usually the State Capital.

9. The electors of each State vote by ballot for President and Vice-President, at least one of whom shall not be an inhabitant of the same State as themselves.

10. They must vote for President and Vice-President on separate ballots.

11. They must make three certificates of all the votes cast for President and Vice President, annexing to each certificate, a certificate of their own election.

12. They must all sign and seal these certificates, and certify on the outside that they contain the votes of their State for President and Vice President.

13. They send one certificate by a special messenger to the President of the Senate; they mail another to him, and the third they

deliver to the Judge of the United States District Court of the district in which they meet.

14. A messenger is allowed twenty-five cents per mile for the distance traveled, and is subject to a fine of $1,000 for neglect of duty.

15. If the two certificates sent to the President of the Senate fail to reach him by the *fourth Monday in January*, he sends a special messenger for the copy deposited with the District Judge.

16. The certificates are opened by the President of the Senate, on the *second Wednesday in February*, in a joint session (**445**) of both houses; the vote is counted by tellers appointed from each house, and is announced by the presiding officer.

17. A majority of all the electoral votes are required to elect.

18. Each State decides contests between rival electors.

19. Each State provides for paying its own electors.

20. No United States Senator or Representative or person holding an office of trust or profit under the government shall be an elector.

21. One elector is taken from each Congressional District and two from the State at large, all being elected on the State ticket.

22. An elector is free to vote for the candidate of the opposite party if he chooses to do so; but thus far in the history of our country, no elector has forsaken his party.

23. Until 1824, electors were usually chosen

by State Legislatures. They are now all chosen by popular vote.

24. Washington (1789, 1793,) received all the electoral votes twice. In 1821, James Monroe received all but one. The one elector had vowed that no one should receive the honor accredited to Washington.

303. Electoral Commission.—A commission appointed by Congress, January, 1877, to settle disputes over the election returns of 1876, from Florida, South Carolina, Louisiana, and Oregon.

2. The commission was made up of five U. S. Senators, five U. S. Representatives, and five U. S. Supreme Judges.

3. Two days before the inauguration, by a vote of eight to seven, the commission decided that Rutherford B. Hayes was elected President over Samuel J. Tilden.

304. Electoral Vote.—The vote of the members of the Electoral College (**302**) for President and Vice-President.

305. Electors-at-Large.—The two Presidential Electors elected from each State, without regard to congressional districts, to represent the two United States Senators of the given State in the Electoral College (**302**).

306. Emancipation Proclamation.—The proclamation of President Lincoln, January 1, 1863, abolishing slavery in those States then in rebellion, and admitting such slaves to the army and navy.

2. About 3,000,000 slaves were freed.

3. Lincoln had issued a preliminary procla-

mation, September 22, 1862, declaring that if any States remained in rebellion January 1, 1863, the slaves in such States would be freed.

4. By the 13th Amendment, ratified December 1865, slavery was forever abolished throughout the jurisdiction of the United States.

307. Embargo.—An order made by a government prohibiting ships of commerce from sailing from its ports, or from particular ports.

2. An embargo act may apply to the departure or to the entering of vessels, or to both; it may apply to vessels and goods generally, or to certain goods alone.

3. A *hostile embargo* is one laid on the vessels of an enemy.

4. A *civil embargo* is one laid on the vessels of the country authorizing it.

5. The United States laid an embargo on all commerce but once, and that in 1807.

308. Embassy or Legation.—A diplomatic agent,—Ambassador, Minister, etc., (**283**)—and all those associated with him; residing at the capital of a foreign country; as the American Legation at London.

309. Embezzlement.—A fraudulent appropriation to one's own use, of the money or goods of another, which were intrusted to the embezzler's care.

2. The crime is unknown to the common law; it depends entirely upon statutory enactments.

310. Embezzler.—One who embezzles (**309**).

311. Enabling Act.—An act passed by Congress upon the petition of a Territory to become a State, authorizing the people of the Territory to frame and adopt a State constitution preparatory to admission into the Union.

2. The act sometimes provides for the admission of the Territory on the proclamation of the President; otherwise it is admitted by another act of Congress.

3. Several Territories adopted State constitutions and were admitted into the Union without enabling acts.

312. Enacting Clause.—The introductory clause of a bill formally expressing the legislative sanction.

313. Enactment.—A law passed by a legislative body. A statute.

314. Engrossed Bill.—A bill that has been plainly written with all its amendments, after its second reading (**78,11-14**), preparatory to final action on its passage.

315. Enrolled Bill.—A bill accurately written on parchment, in a bold hand, after its passage.

316. Entry.—The delivering at the custom-house (**253**), a complete account of a ship's cargo, and obtaining permission to land the goods(**494**).

317. Equity.—(*a*) "The rectification of the law, when, by reason of its universality, it is deficient."—*Aristotle.* (*b*) That branch of jurisprudence (**452**) that is applied to cases for which the law courts afford no plain and adequate remedy.

2. A court of equity (**765,11**) has no juries.

3. It tries no criminal cases.

4. In equity cases, the evidence is all written —depositions.

5. Some States have separate courts of equity and of law; but in most States, the same judge acts in both capacities.

318. Escheat.—The passing of title of real estate to the State by reason of the failure of heirs to claim the same.

319. Evidence.—What is legally submitted to a court as a means of proving or disproving matters of fact.

2. The judge decides what evidence is admissible.

3. The jury decides what weight to attach to evidence.

4. *Direct Evidence* is evidence given on the witness' own personal knowledge of facts.

5. *Circumstantial* or *indirect evidence* is evidence inferred from circumstances, or from facts proven.

6. *To turn States evidence* is to testify against one's accomplices with the express or implied understanding that the witness himself will not be prosecuted.

320. Exceptions.—Objections made by an attorney to rulings of the judge in the course of a trial, and recorded, to be used as grounds for appeal in case of defeat.

321. Excise.—Any indirect tax or duty on imports (**407**) and exports (**332**). A tax on certain home products, as tobacco and spirituous liquors; on national banks, on licenses to deal in certain commodities, etc.

2, Excise duties make up our internal revenue (428).

3. Excise must be uniform throughout the United States.

322. Execution, Writ of.—A writ issued for enforcing the decree of a court in a civil action; as to seize and sell property to satisfy a judgment.

323. Executive.—(*a*) The chief officer who administers the laws of a government; as president, governor, etc.

(*b*) One of the three departments of government, the other two being the legislative and the judicial.

324. Executive Departments.—The Executive Departments of the United States government are eight in number, to-wit:

1. *Department of State*, which looks after the correspondence of the government; it has charge of all the relations· of the government with foreign countries. Its chief officer is the *Secretary of State.* (*See Cabinet,* **116.**)

2. *Department of the Treasury*, which has charge of the financial affairs of the government; of the collection, the safe-keeping and the disbursement of the national revenue; of the national banks, the coinage of money, etc. Its chief officer is the *Secretary of the Treasury*.

(*2*) The *Bureau of Printing and Engraving*, which attends to the printing of all public documents, etc., is under this department.

3. *War Department*, which has charge of the military forces of the government, and of the

signal service (**730**). Its chief officer is the *Secretary of War.*

4. *Department of Justice,* which furnishes legal advice to the President and the Cabinet officers, and has general supervision of United States Marshals and District Attorneys throughout the Union.

(2) Its chief officer is the *Attorney General,* who personally conducts all suits, in the Supreme Court, in which the government is interested.

5. *Post Office Department,* which has charge of the entire postal service of the Union, both at home and with foreign countries.

(2) It establishes post offices, awards contracts for carrying the mail, makes postal treaties (**624**) with other nations, etc.

(3) Its chief officer is the *Post Master General.* He is aided by four *Assistant Post Masters General.* He appoints all Post Masters receiving less than $1,000 per year, the President appointing all others.

6. *Department of the Navy,* which has charge of the navy (**548**) of the government, the construction of war vessels, coast surveys, etc. Its chief officer is the *Secretary of the Navy.*

7. *Department of the Interior,* which has charge of the home affairs of the country, such as (*a*) Pensions, (*b*) the Census, (*c*) Public Lands, (*d*) Patents, (*e*) the Indians, (*f*) Education, (*g*) Public Documents, (*h*) Copyrights, (*i*) Railroads that have received loans or subsidies (**782**) from the United States, (*j*) Surveys,

etc., Its chief officer is the *Secretary of the Interior.*

8. *Department of Agriculture*, which has charge of the interests of agriculture in the United States, collecting and distributing seeds, plants, agricultural information, etc. Its chief officer is the *Secretary of Agriculture.*

9. Other inferior departments set apart to themselves and not represented in the Cabinet are:

(*1*) The *Department of Labor*, which collects and publishes labor statistics.

(*2*) The *Civil Service Commission* (**161**).

(*3*) The *Commission of Fish and Fisheries*, which has charge of the preservation and improvement of fish in the waters of the Union.

(*4*) The *Interstate Commerce Commission* (**431,2**).

325. Executive Mansion.—The White House (**849**).

326. Executor.—A man appointed by the testator himself in his will to carry out its provisions after his death.

2. An executor generally acts as to both personal and real property; an administrator (**11**), only as to personal property.

327. Executrix.—Feminine of Executor(**326**).

328. Exequatur.—An official written recognition of a consul or commercial agent, by the government to which he is accredited, authorizing him to act in his official capacity in that country.

329. Ex Officio.—By virtue of office; as, the Vice-President is *ex officio* President of the

7

Senate.

330. Ex Parte.—From one side only; as an affidavit, which is made by one person without cross-examination.

331. Expatriation.—The renouncing allegiance (**24**) to one's own country.

2. It is required of foreigners (**359**) when they become naturalized (**544**).

332. Exports.—Goods shipped out of a country to other countries.

333. Ex post-facto Law.—A law which makes an act punishable in a manner in which it was not punishable when it was committed. —*U. S. Supreme Court.*

2. The Constitution prohibits Congress and the States from passing such laws.

3. It refers to criminal cases only.

334. Exterritoriality.—Freedom from the jurisdiction of a foreign country while residing within its territorial limits.

2. Diplomatic agents enjoy the privilege of exterritoriality (**283, 10**).

335. Extradition.—The delivery of a fugitive from justice by the authorities of one state or country to the authorities of another having jurisdiction of the crime.

2. The Constitution provides for extradition between the States. The Supreme Court, however, has decided that it is not compulsory.

3. Different countries provide by treaties for extradition.

4. Congress provides that before a fugitive shall be delivered to a foreign country, he shall have a hearing before a Federal or

State Judge, or a Commissioner, who reports the finding to the Secretary of State, who, if a case be made, issues an executive warrant for the delivery of the criminal to the authorities of the foreign government making the demand.

336. Father of the Constitution.—J a m e s Madison.

337. Father of the House.—The member of the House of Representatives who has served the longest time in the House.

338. Federal Courts.—The National judicial system consists of four grades of courts as follows: one *Supreme Court* (**787**), nine *Circuit Courts of Appeals* (**145**), nine *Circuit Courts* (**146**), and over sixty *District Courts*.

2. The Constitution provides for a Supreme Court, but leaves to Congress the establishment of the inferior courts.

3. The orders and processes issuing out of Federal Courts, are binding throughout the entire Union.

4. The Circuit and District Courts have grand juries and trial juries; the others do not.

5. A case must be tried in the State where the cause arises.

6. A Federal Court, as nearly as possible, follows the procedure of the courts of the State in which it is held.

7. Citizens of a Territory or of the District of Columbia cannot bring suits in the Federal Courts; but cases may be appealed from their courts to the Supreme Court.

8. Neither a State nor a citizen can sue the United States without special permission granted by an act of Congress; nor can a citizen sue a State without such permission from its Legislature, and in neither case, can a verdict be enforced.

9. The Federal Courts may try:

. (*1*) All cases arising under the *Constitution the Statutes of Congress, and treaties.*

(*2*) All cases affecting Ambassadors and other foreign Ministers and Consuls.

(*3*) All Admiralty and Maritime cases,— that is, cases affecting naval officers and sea affairs generally.

(*4*) All controversies to which the United States is a party.

(*5*) Controversies between two or more States.

(*6*) Suits between a State and citizens of another State.

(*7*) Suits between citizens of different States.

(*8*) Suits between citizens of the same State claiming lands under grants from different States.

(*9*) Suits between a State or its citizens and a Foreign State or its citizens.

10. Congress also provides for the following *special courts*, which are not Federal Courts: *Consular Courts* (**219**); *Court of the District of Columbia* (**797**,18,5); *Territorial Courts* (**797**,5-8); *Court of Claims* (**241**); *Courts Martial* (**240**); *and Military Courts* (**512**).

339. Federalist, The.—A series of eighty-five essays written by Hamilton, Madison and

Jay, in 1787-88, explaining and defending the Constitution while its ratification, which it aided very much to secure, was yet in question. Hamilton wrote fifty-one, Madison twenty-six, and Jay five; the other three were written by them jointly. They form one of the best commentaries on the Constitution extant.

340. Federal Judges.—There are three grades of Federal Judges—Supreme Judges, Circuit Judges, and District Judges.

2. There are nine Supreme Judges, eighteen Circuit Judges, and over sixty District Judges.

3. All these are appointed by the President with the consent of the Senate.

4. Circuit Judges sit in Circuit Courts of Appeals (**145**) and Circuit Courts.

5. They hold office during good behavior. The only way in which a Federal Judge may be removed from office, is by impeachment.

6. Any Federal Judge seventy years of age, who has served ten years, may retire on full pay.

7. The salaries of Federal Judges are fixed by Congress and may be increased, but not diminished, during their continuance in office.

8. The Chief Justice of the United States receives $10,500 per year; Associate Justices, $10,000 each; Circut Judges $6,000 each; and District Judges, from $3,500 to $5,000 each.

341. Federal Union.—An inseparable union of States forming one grand government of all the people of all the States; as the government of the United States.

342. Federation.—A confederacy. A league of independent allied States.

343. Fee Simple.—An absolute tenure or ownership of real estate.

344. Felony.—A crime punishable by death or by imprisonment in the State prison.

2. *To compound a felony,* is to agree, for a consideration, not to prosecute a felon.

3. The person so agreeing, is liable to indictment.

345. Feudalism.—A system of government in which the king is considered proprietor of all lands, which he distributes among vassals, who let them out to their subordinates, on condition that in each case the inferior renders military duty to the superior.

2. The system flourished in Europe during the latter half of the Middle Ages.

346. Fiat Money.—Paper money not redeemable in specie, and the purchasing power of which depends alone on the *fiat* or decree of the government issuing it.

347. Fiduciary.—One who holds money or property in trust for another; as an administrator, guardian, etc.

348. Filibustering.—(*a*) Delaying legislation by consuming all the time making dilatory motions (**279**).

(*b*) Prosecuting unauthorized military expeditions for the sake of plunder.

349. Fire Eater.—A name applied to one entertaining extreme southern views.

350. Flag.—The Stars and Stripes, the symbol of national sovereignty, was adopted by the Continental Congress June 14th, 1777.

2. It consisted of thirteen stripes and thirteen white stars on a blue field.

3. It was recommended by Washington and a committee appointed by Congress.

4. Mrs. Betty Ross, of Philadelphia, made the first national flag.

5. The Stars and Stripes were used previous to 1777, but with the British union.

6. In 1794, with the addition of two States, the stars and the stripes were increased to fifteen each, and remained so until 1818, when the number of stripes was permanently decreased to thirteen, with a star for each State. There are seven red stripes and six white ones.   *

351. Flag Ship.—The ship that carries the flag of the commanding officer of a fleet, and to which all the other ships must look for orders. It is usually the largest of the fleet.

352. Floating Debt.—Debt not secured by bonds payable at a fixed time.

353. Folk-Moot.—An assembly of the people in general, in colonial days, met to discuss public matters and to try cases.

354. Force Bill.—(*a*) The Bloody Bill (**89**).

(*b*) A bill which became a law in 1870, providing for the enforcement of the 15th Amendment, by punishing all attempts at intimidation and bribery in elections in the reconstructed States. (*c*) A similar but more stringent law of 1871, aimed at the Ku-Kluk-Klan and similar organizations.

355. Foreclosure.—The selling of mortgaged

property according to law.

356. Foreigner.—An alien (**22**).

356a. Foreign Trade.—The trade or commerce carried on with other countries.

357. Fort.—A fortified place where soldiers are lodged.

358. Forgery.—The unlawful making or altering of any writing with intent to defraud another.

2. All the States make forgery a felony (**344**) by statute.

359. Franchise.—(*a*) A particular right or privilege granted by a sovereign (**746**) or a government to individuals.

(*b*) An exemption from ordinary jurisdiction.

360. Franking Privilege.—The privilege of sending matter through the mails without paying postage.

2. It was formerly granted to the President, the Vice-President, Cabinet officers, Delegates (**267**), Members of Congress, and a few others. Also, at different times, to ex-Presidents and widows of Presidents, for life.

3. The privilege was abolished in 1873.

4. By act of 1877, official letters and documents may be sent from the Departments free, and Congressmen may receive and send free, all documents printed by Congress.

5. It is now povided that "The Vice-President, Members and Members-elect of and Delegates and Delegates-elect to Congress shall have the privilege of sending free through the mails, and under their frank, any mail mat-

ter to any Government official or to *any per-son*, correspondence, not exceeding one ounce in weight, *upon official or departmental busi-ness.*" This applies to all officers of the United States government; but it does not apply to *private* mail matter in any case.

361. Fratricide.—(*a*) The crime of killing one's own brother.

(*b*) One who kills his own brother.

362. Fraud.—Intentional deceit wilfully practiced for the purpose of gaining an unlawful or an unfair advantage over another.

2. Deliberate fraud makes a contract invalid.

363. Fraudulent Conveyance.—The transfer of the title of property to one person with intent to defraud another; as to transfer property to defraud a creditor.

364. Free Coinage.—The coining of all standard bullion (**759**) into money for the benefit of the owner of the bullion without charge for coining.

2. In this country, there is free and unlimited coinage of gold, but not of silver.

3. If the bullion deposited be not standard, the actual cost of making it standard, is charged.

4. The mint may, but seldom does, refuse to coin gold bullion of less value than $100.

365. Freedman.—One who has been a slave and has been set free; as the negroes in the United States.

366. Freedman's Bureau.—A bureau established by Congress in 1865 for the relief and edncation of emancipated negroes.

2. It was abandoned in 1870.

367. Freeholder.—One who holds a title to real estate, either in fee simple or for life.

368. Free Silver.—The free coinage (364) of silver.

2. It is not practiced in the United States.

369. Free Trade.—The theory that all commerce should be free and unrestricted by any tariff regulations or requirements whatever.

370. Free Trader.—One who believes in the theory of free trade.

371. Functions of Government.—(*1*) To make laws—legislative; (*2*) to interpret and apply them—judicial; and (*3*) to enforce them—executive.

372. Funding.—The putting of floating debt into the form of interest-bearing bonds with a definite time for maturity.

373. Fusion.—The combining of two or more political parties to carry an election.

374. Gag-Rule.—A rule adopted by Congress in 1836, on motion of John C. Calhoun, to table all anti-slavery petitions without debate.

2. It was abolished in 1844.

375. Gerrymander.—To divide a State into districts in an unnatural way, for the purpose of giving the party controlling the Legislature, an unfair advantage in the election of Representatives.

2. The practice was so called from Elbridge Gerry, who was Governor of Massachusetts when gerrymandering was introduced there, though he opposed it.

3. Gerrymandering gave us the famous "Shoe String District" of Mississippi, 250 miles long and 30 miles wide; and a district in Missouri longer, when measured along its curves, than the State itself.

376. Gifts.—No person holding any office of profit or trust under the United States, shall, without the consent of Congress, accept any present, emolument, office, or title of any kind whatever, from any king, prince or foreign state.

2. Congress has occasionally, by special acts, given such consent.

3. Many valuable gifts have been presented to United States officers, but they could not be accepted, and were turned over to the National Museum.

4. President Van Buren was once presented by a foreign ruler, with some very costly jewels, which are yet to be found in the National Treasury.

377. Gold Bugs.—Those who favor gold as a single standard of money value.

378. Gold Standard.—The legalized use of gold alone as the standard of money values.

379. Government.—Controlling power; the power that makes, interprets and executes the laws; the power that rules a body politic.

2. GENERAL CLASSES $\begin{cases} \text{Democracy,} \\ \text{Monarchy,} \\ \text{Aristocracy.} \end{cases}$

3. A DEMOCRACY is a government in which the supreme ruling power is vested in the people.

(*2*) A *pure* or *absolute democracy* is a government in which all the legal voters, in mass meetings, conduct the affairs of government.

(*3*) *A representative democracy* or *republic*, is a government in which the laws are made, interpreted and executed by *representatives* regularly elected by the people.

4. A MONARCHY is a government in which the ruling power is vested in one person called a monarch.

(*2*) An *absolute monarchy* is a monarchy whose ruler has absolute, unlimited power.

(*3*) A *limited* or *constitutional monarchy* is a monarchy in which the powers of the ruler are limited by a constitution.

(*4*) An *elective monarchy* is a monarchy in which the ruler is elected for life by the people or by representatives.

(*5*) A *hereditary monarchy* is a monarchy in which the ruler inherits the throne.

(*6*) A *despotism* is an absolute monarchy ruled by a cruel tyrant called a despot.

(*7*) A *patriarchy* is a monarchy in which the patriarch or father exercises absolute power over his decendants or tribe. This was the first form of government. Abraham was a patriarchal ruler.

(*8*) A *theocracy* is a monarchy in which the laws are received directly from God. The government of the Hebrews was theocratic in form.

5. An ARISTOCRACY is a government in which the power is exercised by a select few who inherit it; or are appointed to office on

account of their rank or wealth, or both.

6. An *oligarchy* is a government administered by a few self-appointed persons.

7. A *hierarchy* is a government administered by ecclesiastical rulers arranged according to rank.

8. A *plutocracy* is a government administered by the wealthy classes.

9. Some governments are combinations of two or more of the foregoing forms.

380. Government Printing Office.—The printing office under the control of Congress, where the laws of Congress, messages, reports of officers, and, in short, all public printing is done.

2. Formerly, the government hired the public printing done; but the extortionate prices charged forced Congress to establish this office in 1860.

3. A public printer is appointed by the President to superintend the printing and binding done for Congress, for all the deparments, and for the United States Court.

381. Governments of the World.—

1. AFRICA.

Abyssinia,.................................... Kingdom.
Algeria,..............................French Colony.
Cape of Good Hope,................British Colony.
Egypt, ... Empire.
French Kongo,....................French Territory.
German East Africa,...German Protectorate.
Kamerun, ...German Protectorate,
Kongo Free State,................Belgian Colony.
Liberia,...Republic.

Madagascar, ... Kingdom.
Morocco, ...Empire.
Natal, ...British Colony.
Niger Territories, ...British Territories.
Orange Free State, ...Republic.
Free State of E. Africa, ...Portuguese Colony.
Portuguese W. Africa, ...Portuguese Territories.
Senegal, ... French Colony.
Sierra Leone, ...British Colony.
South African Republic, ...Republic.
Togoland, ...German Protectorate.
Tripoli, ...Turkish Province.
Tunis, ...French Protectorate.

2. ASIA.

Afghanistan, ...Empire.
Bhotan, ... Kingdom.
Ceylon, ...British Colony.
China, ... Empire.
Dutch East Indies, ...Dutch Colony.
French India, ...French Colony.
French Indo-China; ....French Dependencies.
Hongkong, ...British Colony.
India, ...Empire.
Japan, ... Empire.
Korea, ... Empire.
Nepal, ... Kingdom.
Oman, ... Empire.
Persia, ... Kingdom.
Philippine Islands, American possessions un-
                            der military rule.
Russia, Asiatic, ... Empire.
Samos, ...Turkish Principality.
Siam, ...Kingdom.
Turkey in Asia, ...Empire.

3. EUROPE.

Andorra. .... Republic.
Austria-Hungary, ... Empire.
Belgium, ...Kingdom.
British Isles, ...Kingdom.
Bulgaria, ... Principality.
Denmark, ... Kingdom.
France, ...Republic.
Germany, ...Empire.
Greece, ... Kingdom.
Italy, ...Kingdom.
Luxemburg, ... Grand Duchy.
Monaco, ...Principality.
Montenegro, ...Principality.
Netherlands, ... Kingdom.
Norway, ... Kingdom.
Portugal, ... Kingdom.
Roumania, ... Kingdom.
Russia, ... Empire.
San Marino, ... Republic.
Servia, ...Kingdom.
Spain, ... Kingdom.
Sweden, ... Kingdom.
Switzerland, ... Republic.
Turkey, ...Empire.

4. NORTH AMERICA.

Bahamas, ...British Colony.
Barbadoes, ...British Colony.
Bermuda, ... British Colony.
Canada, ...British Colony.
Costa Rica, ... Republic.
Cuba,...... Independent, under U. S. protection.
Guatemala, ... Republic.
Haiti................................Republic.

Honduras, ... Republic.
Honduras, British, ... British Colony.
Jamaica, ... British Colony.
Mexico, ... Republic.
Newfoundland, ...British Colony.
Nicaragua, ... Republic.
Puerto Rico, American possession under military rule.
Salvador, ...Republic.
Santo Domingo, ... Republic.
United States, ...Republic.

5. OCEANICA.

Bismarck Archipelago, German Protectorate.
Fiji, ... British Colony.
Hawaii. United States possession with provisional government.
Kaiser Wilhelm's Land,   German Protectorate.
Marshall Islands, ... German Protectorate.
New Caledonia, ... French Colony.
New Guinea, ...British Colony.
New Hebrides, ... Independent.
New South Wales, ...British Colony.
New Zealand, ... British Colony.
Queensland, ...British Colony.
Samoa, ...Kingdom.
Society Islands, ...French Colony.
Solomon Islands, ...German Protectorate.
South Australia, ... British Colony.
Tasmania, ...British Colony.
Tonga, ... Kingdom.
Victoria, ...British Colony.
Western Australia, ...British Colony.

6. SOUTH AMERICA.

Argentine Republic, ... Republic.
Bolivia, ... Republic.
Brazil, ...Republic.
Chili, ... Republic.
Colombia, ... Republic.
Ecuador, ... Republic.
Guiana, British, ...British Colony.
Guiana, Dutch, ... Dutch Colony.
Guiana, French, ... French Colony.
Paraguay, ... Republic.
Peru, ...Republic.
Uruguay, ... Republic.
Venezuela, ...Republic.

382. Governor.—The chief executive officer of a State or a Territory.

2. All State Governors are elected by direct vote. Territorial Governors are appointed by the President (**797,2**).

3. In general, the duties and powers of a Governor in his State, are identical with those of the President of the United States (**636**).

383. Grand Jury.—A jury that inquires into accusations of crime against persons, and determines whether the evidence against them warrants a new trial or not.

2. It acts only in criminal cases.

3. Its sessions are secret.

4. It never tries cases.

5. It makes indictments (**415**) or presentments (**630**).

6. It is called in each county several times a year.

7. It usually requires twelve to make an in-

8

dictment.

8. The number of grand jurors as a rule varies in the different States from twelve to twenty-three. Oregon has but *seven*.

9. No person, except in the army or navy, or in the militia in active service, can be tried for a grave crime against the United States without first being indicted(415). Most State constitutions make the same provision.

10. Petty State crimes may be tried without indictment.

11. The United States Supreme Court holds that the first ten Amendments do not apply to the States; hence States may try State crimes without indictment by a grand jury.

12. A few States have no grand juries; in some, grand juries are summoned only upon the request of the court.

13. No witness for the accused is examined by the grand jury.

14. The judge appoints the foreman, or the jury elects one.

15. The grand jury of the United States Circuit Court has jurisdiction over crimes committed in any of the States comprising the circuit; that of a United States District Court acts for the district.

383a. Grand Model.—The fundamental Constitution of Carolina. A very elaborate constitution framed by John Lock and Lord Shaftsbury (1669) for the government of Carolina (now North and South Carolina.)

2. They pronounced it the most perfect work of the kind that ever emanated from

the human mind, and said that it would continue to be the sacred and unalterable form and rule of government forever.

3. It gave to the nobility all power, and to the common people nothing, and of course it was an utter failure.

384. Greenbacks.—The popular name for the legal tender treasury notes or promises to pay money, issued during the Civil War. They depreciated greatly until 1879, when they were made redeemable in gold and silver.

385. Guardian.—One who has legal charge of the person and property of another.

386. Guerrillas.—Small maurauding bands under a leader or chief, who carry on petty and irregular warfare.

2. J. H. Morgan was a most noted guerrilla chief of the Civil War.

3. The practice originated in Spain.

387. Guild.—A privileged association of men of the same occupation, which marked society lines in early days, when to be a citizen, one must belong to a guild, the door to which was long apprenticeship.

388. Habeas Corpus.—A writ issued by a Judge, commanding a person holding another in custody, to bring the prisoner before him that he may examine into the legality of the imprisonment.

5. If he find the imprisonment illegal, he will release the prisoner; otherwise he will send him back to prison.

3. The Judge does not try the case under the writ of *habeas corpus*; he merely inquires into

the legality of the imprisonment.

4. To secure a writ of *habeas corpus*, the prisoner, or some person for him, applies to a Judge for a writ, making oath that the imprisonment is illegal, and setting forth the facts in the case.

5. It is a writ of right, and not a writ of course; and the Judge will not issue it, if to his mind, the facts set forth in the case do not warrant it.

6. The privilege of the writ of *habeas corpus* shall not be suspended unless when, in cases of rebellion or invasion, the public safety may require it.

7. The Constitution does not state who shall have the power to suspend the privilege of the writ. It was first suspended during the Civil War (1861), by President Lincoln.

8. Then, in 1861, Congress suspended it in nine counties in South Carolina in order to suppress the Ku-Klux Klan.

9. The object of the writ is to prevent unlawful imprisonment. It is the great safeguard of personal liberty. It distinguishes the free government from the despotism (**278**).

389. Hard Cider Campaign.—The presidential campaign of 1840.

2. It is also called the *Log Cabin Campaign.*

390. High Seas.—That part of the ocean common to all nations, and lying beyond three miles from the coast line.

391. Holograph or Olograph.—Any document, as a deed, letter, will, etc., written entirely by the hand of the person whose thoughts, wishes or intentions it sets forth; as a holographic will, etc.

392. Home Department.—Department of the Interior (323 7).

393. Homestead Law.—A law passed in 1862, giving any citizen 160 acres of public land free, on the payment of certain small fees, and five years of continuous residence on the land.

394. Homicide.—The killing of one human being by another.

2. Homicide may be *feloneous*, as murder or manslaughter; *excusable* and in self-defense, as in the defense of property, etc; or *justifiable*, as the legal execution of a criminal.

395. House of Burgesses.—The legislative body of Virginia from 1619 to 1774.

2. It was the first representative body in America.

396. House of Commons.—The lower house of the British Parliament, consisting of 670 representatives elected for a term of seven years, unless Parliament be sooner dissolved by royal proclamation, which has always happened thus far.

2. Members receive no pay.

3. The Commons elect their own Speaker and other officers.

4. Forty members constitute a quorum (662).

5. The Commons virtually control legislation in general.

6. Of the 670 members, England elects 465; Scotland, 72; Wales, 30; and Ireland, 103.

7. All revenue bills must originate in the

House of Commons.

397. House of Lords.—The upper house of the British Parliament, composed of the whole body of 489 English peers (588); 16 Scottish representative peers elected by the whole body of Scotch peers, (of whom there are 85,) to serve for one term; 28 Irish representative peers elected by the 177 peers of Ireland, to serve for life; and the two Archbishops and 24 Bishops of England, called *lords spiritual*, who hold seats in Parliament by virtue of their offices, the same as English peers—in all, 559 members at present.

2. Members receive no pay.

3. The number of Scottish and Irish peers is limited by statute.

4. The Lord Chancellor of England is always Speaker of the House of Lords.

5. Though the House of Lords is in theory co-equal with the House of Commons, it is in reality much inferior in authority.

398. House of Representatives.—The lower and more numerous branch of Congress; and in some States, the name applied to the lower branch of the State Legislature.

399. House of Representatives, U. S.—The lower and more numerous house of Congress.

2. It is (1899) composed of 357 members.

3. The first House consisted of 65 members.

4. It has the sole power of impeachment (**404**).

5. All bills for raising revenue must originate in the House; but the Senate may propose, or concur in, amendments as in other bills.

6. A vacancy in a State's representation in the House is filled by a special election called by the Governor of that State.

7. The House elects a President in case the Eletors fail to do so (**636,3**).

8. The Clerk of the previous House presides until the Speaker is elected. If he can not preside, the Sergeant-at-Arms does so.

9. The presiding officer is addressed as "Mr. Speaker," and is elected by the House from its own members.

10. The Speaker can therefore vote on all questions.

11. The House also elects a Clerk, a Sergeant-at-Arms, a Doorkeeper, a Post Master and a Chaplain, none of which are members.

12. A very large number of subordinate officers are appointed to assist these.

13. The length of speeches in the House is limited by the House rules.

14. The House makes its own rules of procedure.

15. An entirely new House is elected every two years.

16. A member, (usually the "Father of the House,") administers the oath of office to the Speaker, who in turn administers it to the other officers of the House and to the other Representatives by States.

17. Each daily session of the House is opened with prayer.

18. The House can not adjourn for more than three days nor to another place of meeting without the consent of the Senate.

19. It is the judge of the elections, returns and qualifications of its own members.

20. It has concurrent jurisdiction with the Senate in enacting laws.

21. A yea and nay vote (859) must be taken if one-fifth of the members present demand it.

22. The committees of the House (187,7) are appointed by the Speaker, and not elected as in the Senate.

23. By a rule of the House, 15 members including the Speaker can compel the attendance of absent members.

24. A majority of the members constitutes a quorum (662).

25. The House represents the *National* idea in our government—the people; while the Senate represents the *Federal* idea—the States.

400. Hundred.—The smallest judicial district of England, made up of townships.

2. It was supposed to contain a hundred families, or to furnish a hundred warriors; hence its name.

3. It has lost its judicial element, and the name now applies only to the district.

4. The term was transplanted to America, and one State—Delaware—still retains it; but it means the same as township there.

401. Hundred Court or Hundred Moot.—T h e court of the Hundred; a representative body composed of the lords of the lands in the Hundred, with the reeve, the parish priest, and the "four best men" from each township.

402. Hundredman.—Chief magistrate of the

Hundred; called later, the high constable.

493. Immunes.—A term applied to volunteer soldiers in the Spanish-American War who, having had the yellow fever, or having been exposed to it without taking it, were considered proof against the fever and enjoyed immunity from adverse climatic conditions of the tropics.

404. Impeachment.—A formal accusation or charge brought against a public officer for "treason, bribery, or other high crimes and misdemeanors."

2. In Congress, the House of Representatives has the sole power of impeachment, and proceeds as follows:

3. Upon formal complaint to the House, an investigating committee is appointed. If it reports in favor of impeachment, the House votes on the question, and if a majority favor impeachment, *articles of impeachment* are prepared, and a committee is appointed to prosecute the case before the Senate.

4. The Senate has sole power to try impeachments.

5. When sitting for the purpose, Senators must be under special oath or affirmation.

6. When the President of the United States is tried, the Chief Justice presides; because the Vice President is an interested party.

7. It requires a two-thirds vote of the members present to convict.

8. Judgment in case of impeachment shall not extend further than to removal from office, and disqualification to hold and enjoy any

office of honor, trust, or profit under the United States.

9. But the party convicted shall, nevertheless, be liable and subject to indictment, trial, judgment and punishment, according to law.

10. The judgment need not necessarily extend to both removal and disqualification.

11. The President, Vice-President, and all civil officers of the United States, are liable to impeachment.

12. Congressmen are not considered civil officers and therefore can not be impeached.

13. The President can not pardon or reprieve in cases of impeachment; but he can pardon and reprieve in all other cases against the United States.

14. In the case of State officers, the lower House of the State Legislature impeaches, and the State Senate tries the impeachment.

405. Imperialism.—The spirit or desire to acquire an empire; imperial power or government.

406. Implied Powers of Congress.—Those powers only that are necessary to carry out the express powers. (See *Elastic Clause*, **297**.)

407. Imports.—Goods shipped into a country from other countries.

408. Impost.—A tax or duty. As used in the Constitution, a duty on imported goods.

409. Impressment.—The act of seizing men and of forcing them into public service; as the British impressment of American seamen, which was one cause of the War of 1812.

410. Inauguration.—The act of introducing

into office with formal ceremonies. (*Inauguration of President and Vice-President*, **636,26**).

411. Income Tax.—A certain per cent levied upon all annual incomes exceeding a certain amount.

2. Such a tax was collected but once, (1861-71) in which case the Supreme Court decided that it was not a direct tax within the meaning of the Constitution.

3. In 1894, an income tax was laid for a second time, but the Supreme Court, by a vote of five to four, pronounced it unconstitutional in its proposed form, on the ground that it was a direct tax and that therefore it had to be apportioned among the States according to population (**792,7**).

412. Indemnity.—Compensation for loss or injury sustained, or security against loss or damage; as, in war, the successful nation may require the conquered power to pay an indemnity.

413. Indenture.—A written agreement between two or more parties, of which, each party usually retains a copy.

414. Independence Hall.—The hall in Philadelphia where the Declaration of Independence was sighed, July 4th, 1776.

415. Indictment.—A formal written accusation of crime made by a grand jury (**383**) against a certain person.

2. The prosecuting officer frames a bill of indictment (**82**) and sends it to the grand jury, who examine witnesses (**855**), and the foreman (**383,13**) writes across it: "a true bill," if the

jury agrees to the indictment: otherwise, he indorses it "not found."

3. No person in civil life can be tried for a capital or otherwise infamous crime against the United States, except on indictment.

4. State criminals may be tried without indictment by a grand jury.

416. Indorsement.—The writing on the back of a note or other negotiable paper transferring it to some one else.

2. *Indorsement in full,*—the writing of one's name on the back of a note, etc., with an order to pay to some particular person.

3. *Indorsement in blank,*—the writing of one's name simply, on the back of a note, check, etc., by which the paper is made payable to the bearer.

417. Indorser.—One who writes his name on the back of a note, check, draft, order, etc., as a receipt, or as a guarantee of payment.

2. An indorser must be notified of the nonpayment of an obligation when it becomes due, or his liability ceases.

418. Infamous Crime.—Held by the Supreme Court to be a crime punishable by imprisonment at hard labor for a number of years.

419. Infant.—Any person not of legal age; a minor.

420. Infanticide.—(*a*) The killing of a young child.

(*b*) A child murderer.

421. Infantry.—A body of foot soldiers.

422. Initiative.—The right to originate or propose laws or measures.

2. The House of Representatives possesses the initiative in the case of revenue bills (**696**).

3. In some cantons in Switzerland, a certain number of people may propose laws, which must be submitted to the popular vote for ratification or rejection.

423. Injunction.—A writ issued by a court of equity (**765,11**), (sometimes by a court of law) requiring a person or persons to do, or not to do, a certain thing; usually the latter.

424. Inquest.—A judicial inquiry or legal examination into any civil or criminal matter.

2. A *coroner's inquest* is an inquiry held by a coroner (**230**) before a jury, to inquire into the cause of a sudden or mysterious death.

3. An *inquest of office* is an inquiry before a jury at the instance of a proper officer into matters involving the rights of the State.

4. *Grand inquest* is a term sometimes applied to the grand jury.

425. Insolvent.—A bankrupt (**73**); one who is unable to pay his debts as they become due.

426. Insurrection.—An open attempt by individuals, to prevent the enforcement of law, by force of arms, with no intention to overthrow the government.

427. Intercitizenship.—The mutual right of the citizens of each State "to all privileges and immunities of citizens of the several States."

428. Internal Revenue.—That part of the national revenue that is derived from excise duties (**321**).

2. For the collection of internal revenue, the

whole country is divided into collection districts, and a Collector of Internal Revenue is appointed by the President, for each district.

429. International Copyright.—The right of citizens of one country to secure copyrights in another as provided for by treaty (**817**).

430. International Law or The Law of Nations.—The rules and customs recognized by civilized nations as regulating their mutual intercourse.

2. It differs from all other law in that it is not the expression of a controlling will, and can not therefore be enforced except by war.

3. Questions of dispute arising under international law, are now usually settled by arbitration (**39**).

431. Inter-State Commerce Act.—An act passed by Congress in 1887, to regulate inter-state commerce by railroads and all inter-state common carriers. It does not affect railroads lying wholly within a State.

2. The provisions of the act are carried out by the *Inter-State Commerce Commission* appointed for that purpose.

432. Intestate.—One who dies without making a valid will.

433. Intimidation.—The act of keeping voters from the polls (**617**) by means of threats, etc.

434. Iron-Clad Oath.—A special rigid oath of office prescribed by Congress in 1862, in accordance with Sec. 3, Amendment 14, of the Constitution, as a safeguard against the holding of office by secessionists or those who might thereafter prove disloyal to the government.

435. Invisible Empire or White League.— The Ku-Klux Klan (461).

436. Jail.—A county or local prison.

437. Jeopardy.—Danger; peril; exposure to punishment.

2. A person cannot be tried or put in jeopardy a second time for the same crime.

438. Jingo.—One who advocates a spirited domineering policy in foreign affairs.

2. It was in this sense first applied to the British party that favored the Franco-Russian War of 1877-8.

439. Jobbery.—The practice of turning official power to private advantage; as appointing certain men to office, awarding public contracts, etc., for money or personal favors of some kind.

440. Joint Ballot.—A ballot cast jointly by two distinct assemblies voting together as one body (445).

441. Joint Committee.—A committee provided for by a joint resolution, and composed of members of both branches of a legislative body.

442. Joint Meeting.—A meeting of two distinct bodies organized as one.

443. Joint Resolution.—A resolution (691) adopted by the concurrent vote of both branches of a legislative assembly, and having the force of law.

444. Joint Rule.—A rule of procedure adopted by the concurrent vote of both branches of a legislative assembly.

445. Joint Session.—A joint meeting of two distinct assemblies organized as one body.

446. Joint Stock Company.—An incorporated company whose capital is divided into shares of a given amount, which are transferable at the will of the owners.

447. Judge-Advocate-General.—The chief officer of the bureau of military justice in the War Department, having the rank of Brigadier General.

(*b*) The chief of the bureau of justice in the Navy, having the rank of Colonel.

448. Judgment.—The decision of a court of justice.

449. Judiciary.—(*a*) One of the three departments of Government, in which the judicial power is vested.

(*b*) The whole system of courts of justice of a state or nation.

450. Junto.—A cabal (115).

451. Jurisdiction.—The legal authority or power of a court to hear and determine a case.

2. *Original Jurisdiction* is the right or power of a court to hear and determine a cause in the first instance.

3. *Appellate Jurisdiction* is the right or power of a court to hear and determine a cause after it has been tried in a lower court.

452. Jurisprudence.—The science of law as administered in courts of justice.

453. Jury.—A body of men legally selected and sworn to inquire into any matter of fact and render a true verdict (**834**) according to the evidence given in the case, and the law, as interpreted by the judge.

Grand Jury (**383**); *Petit* or *Trial Jury* (**595**); *Justice's Jury* (**456**); *Coroner's Jury* (**231**); *Struck Jury* (**774**).

454. Justice of the Peace.—A judicial officer of the lowest grade, having local jurisdiction in minor civil and criminal cases.

2. In most States, Justices of the Peace are elected by the voters of their magisterial districts; in a few, they are appointed by the Governor.

3. Their term of office varies in the different States, from one to seven years.

4. A Justice has jurisdiction throughout his county.

5. He issues warrants for the arrest of offenders, and tries petty criminal cases; and civil cases when the amount involved does not exceed a certain amount, varying in the different States. He examines and acquits, or remands for trial in a higher court, those charged with grave offenses. He takes acknowledgments (9), sometimes acts as coroner, and has other duties which vary in the different States.

455. Justice's Court.—A court presided over by a Justice of the Peace,—the oldest court we have.

456. Justice's Jury.—A jury sworn to truly decide cases in a Justice's court.

2. It consists of six members.

3. In civil suits where the amount in controversy exceeds $20, either party may demand a jury.

9

457. Kansas-Nebraska Bill.—A bill passed by Congress May 22nd, 1854, organizing Kansas and Nebraska as separate Territories and repealing the Missouri Compromise of 1820, so far as it related to them, leaving the question of slavery to be decided by the Territories respectively. The bill did much to hasten the war.

458. Kidnap.—To steal a human being; to forcibly carry away a human being, as for purposes of slavery, etc.

459. Kitchen Cabinet.—A select number of President Jackson's intimate friends who were accredited with having more influence with him than his official Cabinet had.

460. Knifing.—Secret and treacherous opposition to a candidate by persons of his own party who pretend to support him.

461. Ku-Klux Klan.—A secret political organization of ex-Confederate soldiers in the South immediately after the Civil War (1868-71).

2. Its pretended object was to preserve law and order, but its real object was to repress the political power of the negroes.

3. In 1871, Congress passed the Ku-Klux Bill suspending the writ of *habeas corpus* in nine counties in South Carolina, called out the militia, and brought the combination to an end.

462. Landslide.—An unexpected overwhelming party majority given in an election.

463. Larceny.—Theft. The unlawful taking and carrying away by one person, of the personal property of another, with intent to permanently deprive the owner of the same without his consent.

2. Personal property alone is the subject of larceny.

3. If the consent of the owner is obtained even by fraud, there is no larceny.

4. *Grand larceny* is the taking of the personal property of another, of or above a certain amount fixed by statute and varying in the different States. It is made a felony by statute.

5. *Petit larceny* is the taking of the personal property of another of a value less than that prescribed by statute for grand larceny.

6. It is made a misdemeanor (523) by statute.

7. *Compound larceny* is larceny committed under aggravating circumstances; as to take goods directly from a house, or from the person of the owner.

8. *Simple larceny* is larceny attended by no aggravating circumstances.

464. Law.—A rule of conduct established by a controlling will.

Civil law (154); *Commercial law* (181); *Common law* (189); *Criminal law* (249); *Club law* (167); *International law* (430); *Lynch law* (488); *Marine or Maritime law* (499); *Martial law* (502); *Military law* (513); *Municipal law* (536); *Statute law* (770).

465. Leading Question.—A question so framed as to suggest the answer desired or expected.

2. Such questions are permitted in the cross-

examination (**250**) of witnesses, but are not allowed in the examination in chief.

466. League.—An alliance of two or more nations, states or colonies, for general or special governmental purposes.

2. The first league formed in this country was the League of the New England Colonies, or "The United Colonies of New England" (Massachusetts, Connecticut, Plymouth, and New Haven) of 1643, for mutual protection against the Dutch, French and Indians.

3. This League lasted 41 years, and its affairs were administered by an Assembly composed of two commissioners from each Colony.

467. Lease.—The letting of lands and houses for a term of years, for life, or at will, for a fixed compensation.

(*a*) The *lessor* is the person who gives the lease.

(*b*) *Lessee*, the person who takes the lease.

468. Legacy.—Property willed by one person to another; a bequest.

469. Legal Tender.—The kind of money that a debtor may legally tender, and a creditor is required by law to accept, in payment of a debt.

2. No foreign money is a legal tender in the United States.

3. The United States may and does make paper money a legal tender; but a State may not do so, though if it chooses, it may make any gold or silver coin legal tender in any amount greater than that prescribed by the United States laws.

470. Legatee.—One to whom property is left by will.

471. Legator.—A testator; one who leaves property to another by will.

472. Legislation.—The act or process of making laws (**464**).

473. Legislature.—The supreme law-making body of a State.

2. All the State Legislatures are composed of two houses, the lower house being variously named in different States.

3. Qualifications of members differ in the different States.

4. Generally, senators serve for a longer term, and represent larger districts than representatives. In a few States, the terms are the same; and in some, all members—Senators and Representatives are elected by counties.

5. The Senate always has fewer members than the House.

6. The Legislature meets at the State Capital.

7. The legislative powers of the Legislature, are limited by the Federal Constitution, the laws of Congress, and the State Constitution.

474. Letters of Administration.—The written authority of an administrator given by the proper officer or court to administer the goods of the deceased.

475. Letters of Marque (*boundary*) **and Reprisal** (*act of retaliation*).—Commissions issued by the government to private individuals authorizing them to go beyond the boundary of their country and to seize the property or sub-

jects of another nation, or the property of its
subjects, in retaliation for injuries committed
by such nation.

2. Such letters are sanctioned by the law of
nations (430).

3. Congress alone can authorize the President to issue letters of marque and reprisal.
The power is denied to the States.

4. Property thus taken belongs to those taking it.

5. Such letters were granted in the Revolutionary War, and authorized, but not issued, in the Civil War.

476. Letters Patent.—The official documents
granting a patent (581) to an inventor.

477. Letters Testamentary.—Written authority given to an executor by the proper officer
after a will has been probated, authorizing
him to act.

478. Libel.—A false, malicious publication
that injures another person in his reputation
or business, or holds him up to public ridi-
cule or contempt.

2. It also includes any blasphemous, treasonable, or immoral publication.

3. The publication may be by writing, printing, pictures, or any sign.

4. Libel is an indictable offense, and the person injured may also recover damages in a
civil suit (151).

5. Libel differs from slander in being published, while the latter is uttered orally (738).

479. Liberty.—The enjoyment of one's
rights.

480. License.—Legal authority to do that which would otherwise be illegal.

481. Lien.—A legal claim upon real or personal property of another until a debt is paid.

482. Lieutenant-Governor.—A Vice-Governor elected in many of the States.

2. He is the presiding officer of the State Senate, and acts as Governor in case of the absence or disability of that officer.

3. The following States have no Lieutenant-Governors: Alabama, Arkansas, Delaware, Georgia, Maine, Maryland, New Hampshire, New Jersey, Oregon, Tennessee and West Virginia.

483. Lobbyists, Lobby Members, or the Third House.—Persons who frequent the lobbies of legislative halls for the purpose of influencing legislation by inducing members, with money, with argument, or otherwise, to vote for or against certain special bills.

2. Some expert professional lobbyists command exorbitant salaries—salaries larger than the members themselves receive.

484. Local Government.—When the Constitution was adopted there were three types of local government—

(1) The *town* or township type of New England, where the town was the political unit, and the voters in mass meetings made laws and elected officers. The towns were represented in the State Legislature.

(2) The *county* type of the Southern States, where the county was the political unit. The county was represented in the State Legislat-

ure.

(3) The *mixed* type of the Middle States, which was a combination of the town and county types.

(4) All these types still exist.

485. Local Option.—The right of certain districts, as a town, city, magisterial district, or county, to determine by popular vote or by local legislation, whether certain things shall be permitted or prohibited; as the sale of intoxicating liquors, certain stock regulations, etc.

486. Log-Rolling.—An exchange of political favors by officials; as a vote for a vote, influence for influence, etc.

487. Loyalists or Tories.—Those in the thirteen colonies who favored the king and sought to aid him prior to, and during, the Revolution.

488. Lynch-Law.—The punishing of criminals by private citizens without due process of law.

2. Sometimes the lynchers organize a court of their own, and go through the form of a trial.

3. The term is supposed to have originated from a Virginian named Lynch, who was a law unto himself.

489. Machine, Political.—A political ring (612).

490. Magna Charta or Great Charter.—A document that the lords, barons and clergy forced King John to sign in 1215.

2. It secured to the English people all the

rights and privileges they claimed, prominent among which, were taxation by a representative body, and absolute right to life, liberty and property, "save by legal judgment of their peers."

491. Majority Vote.—More than half of all the votes cast in an election.

492. Malefactor.—A criminal.

493. Mandamus.—A writ issued by a superior court, commanding an inferior court, an officer or a corporation, to perform some specific duty named therein.

494. Manifest. (*a*) An invoice of the cargo of goods to be examined by custom-house officials.

(*b*) A manifesto.

495. Manifesto.—The public written declaration issued by a ruler or government setting forth his or its intentions, motives or opinions in regard to some public matter; as a manifesto stating intentions of engaging in war, and the reasons therefor.

496. Manor.—A district or landed estate under the jurisdiction of a lord: transplanted into some of the colonies from England; but it has disappeared.

497. Manslaughter.—The unlawful killing of a human being without malice either express or implied and without excuse, as through negligence.

498. Marine.—A soldier serving in the navy.

499. Maritime or Marine Law.—The law of the sea; it applies to ships, seamen, navigation, and affairs of the sea and public waters generally.

500. Maritime Rights.—The right of vessels of all nations to navigate the high seas (390) without hindrance, subject only to international law.

2. Vessels in the territorial waters (796) of any country are subject to its laws.

501. Marshal.—(*a*) The ministerial officer of a federal court, with duties similar to those of a sheriff. One is appointed by the President for each federal judicial circuit.

(*b*) The chief public officer in some cities.

502. Martial Law.—The law of war. The law that regulates the conduct of men in the Army and Navy.

503. Mason and Dixon's Line.—A line run from the Delaware River westward 244 miles, by Charles Mason and Jeremiah Dixon, marking the boundary between Maryland and Pennsylvania.

2. Later, it became famous as the boundary line between the free States and the slave States.

504. Mass Convention.— A convention of all the legal voters of the party who choose to attend, each one having a voice in the proceedings.

505. Matricide.—The murder of a mother by her child, or one who murders his mother.

506. Mayflower Compact.—T h e c o m p a c t made by the Pilgrim Fathers on board the Mayflower before landing, November 11, 1620, binding themselves into a "civil body politic" and agreeing to make and obey "just and equal" laws as such. It was the first expression of the American idea that "governments derive their just powers from the consent of the governed."

507. Mayor.—The executive officer of a municipal corporation;-of a city, town or village.

508. Mecklenburg Resolutions.—Resolutions passed by a convention in Mecklenburg County North Carolina, May 20th, 1775, favoring independence from Great Britain, and declaring the independence of the county named.

509. Member of Congress.—A congressman (203).

510. Memorial.—(*a*) A written reminder of some person or event.

(*b*) A written document addressed to a legislative or other body or to a government, calling attention to facts set forth therein.

511. Military Academy.—Established by Congress, at West Point, New York, in 1802.

2. It educates persons to be army officers.

3. Applicants must be at least 17, and not over 22, years old, of sound body, and able to pass the required examination in reading, writing, orthography, arithmetic, grammar, geography and United States history.

4. The total number of students is 371—one for each Representative and Delegate in Congress, and the President appoints one for the District of Columbia, and ten at large.

5. The Secretary of War appoints students upon the recommendations of Representatives.

6. The course is four years; students receive

$540 per year to pay expenses, and on graduation, are commissioned second lieutenants in the army.

7. Appointees must agree to serve the United States eight years from the time they enter the Academy.

512. Military Court.—A court organized to act in place of a regular court in a section engaged in active warfare, where the regular court can not perform its usual duties.

513. Military Law.—The law prescribed by the Civil Government for the control of affairs in the sections of country actually engaged in war, where the regular courts can not properly perform their duties.

514. Militia.—The citizen soldiers as distinguished from the regular army (**44,2**).

2. The militia consists of all able men between 18 and 45 years of age who are citizens or who have declared their intentions to become citizens, except government and court officers, ministers, teachers, physicians, firemen, etc.

3. The *organized militia* are those organized under State or United States laws.

4. The *unorganized militia* consists of that portion of militia not already organized, officered and equipped.

5. Congress provides for organizing, arming and disciplining the State or organized militia, but the States have the right to appoint their officers and drill them according to the discipline prescribed by Congress.

6. The Governor is Commander-in-Chief of the state militia, and may call them out to quell

riots, etc.

7. The President may call them or any of them out—

(*1*) To execute the laws of the United States.

(*2*) To suppress insurrections, or,

(*3*) To repel invasions. When they are thus called out, he is Commander-in-Chief.

8. The militia have been called out by the President four times; during the Whiskey insurrection of 1794, the war of 1812, the Civil war, and the Spanish-American War of 1898.

9. When the President wants the militia, he calls on the Governors of the different States, and if the required number is not furnished, the government drafts enough men to make up the deficiency.

10. The militia numbered, (January 1st, 1898) 10,139,788; of which number 1,391, staff officers and 113,460 belonged to the organized militia.

515. Ministerial Officer.—One that waits upon, or ministers to, a court or other body.

516. Ministers.—The officers of the Diplomatic Service (**283**). They represent the United States in foreign countries in a political capacity.

517. Minor.—Any person not of legal age; an infant.

518. Minor Coin.—Small coin not made of silver.

2. They are legal tender for any sum not exceeding twenty-five cents.

519. Minority President.—A President who, though he receives a majority of the Electoral votes, yet receives but a minority of the popular vote.

5. Several Presidents have been so elected.

520. Minority Representation.—A representation secured by the minority by means of the cumulative vote (**251**); as in Illinois, where three representatives to the Legislature are elected from each district, and each voter may vote for two or three candidates, or give his three votes to one of them.

521. Minority Vote.—Fewer than half of all the votes cast.

522. Mint.—A place where money is coined by authority of law.

2. Our principal mint is at Philadelphia, with branch mints at Carson City, New Orleans, Sanfrancisco and Denver.

523. Misdemeanor.—A minor crime punishable by fine, by imprisonment in the county jail, or by both.

524. Missouri Compromise.—An Act of Congress, March, 1820, admitting Missouri as a slave State, and providing that forever thereafter no more slave States should be admitted north of parallel 36° 30′,—the southern boundary line of Missouri.

2. It was repealed by the Kansas-Nebraska Bill (**457**), in 1854.

525. Mob.—A riotous or unlawful assembly.

526. Mobilize.—To put new troops in readiness for active service when war is imminent.

527. Moderator.—The presiding officer of an assembly.

528. Money.—Anything stamped by public authority and lawfully used as a medium of exchange.

529. Monometallism.—The use of but one metal, as gold or silver, as the money-standard of a country.

2. The United States has monometallism, gold being the standard.

530. Monopoly.—The sole right, power or privilege of dealing in any kind of goods.

531. Monroe Doctrine.—The doctrine set forth in President Monroe's message, 1823; in substance, "America for Americans."

2. It was occasioned by Russia, Prussia, France and Austria's supposed intention to aid Spain reconquer Mexico and several South American States that had thrown off Spanish rule.

532. Moot Court.—A mock court, where fictitious cases are tried for amusement or practice.

533. Mortgage.—An instrument conveying real or personal property to secure the payment of a debt, upon the payment of which it becomes void.

2. A *chattel mortgage* is a mortgage on personal property.

534. Motion.—A proposal formally made in a deliberative body.

535. Municipal Government.—The local government of a city or of a chartered town or village (**148**).

536. Municipal Law.—(*a*) A rule of civil conduct prescribed by the supreme power of the state.—*Blackstone*.

(*b*) Especially the local laws of a city or

town.

537. Murder.—The unlawful killing of a human being with malice aforethought either express or implied.

538. Mutiny.—A forcible resistance to established authority, especially in the army and on board vessels at sea.

539. Nation.—A body politic (**94**); the whole body of inhabitants of a country organized under one independent government.

540. National Bank.—A bank authorized by the United States laws, by which it is granted certain privileges.

2. Five or more persons, with a capital of not less than $50,000, may organize a national bank, if they invest that sum in United States bonds and deposit the same with the treasurer of the United States.

3. They can issue national bank bills to the amount of ninety per cent. of the capital. These bills, being secured by the bonds, are good anywhere, even though the bank fail.

4. Such banks draw interest on the bonds and on the money loaned, at the same time.

541. National Guard.—The organized militia of the several States, numbering (January 1st. 1898). 113,460.

2. The President, through the Governors, may call them out—

(1) To execute the laws of the United States.

(2) To supress insurrections.

(3) To repel invasions.

3. The Governors may call them out for duty as above, within their respective States.

542. National Prisons.—The United States has no national prisons. By courtesy of the States and counties, federal prisoners are permitted to be confined in their prisons.

543. Nativism.—The doctrine that the government should be in the hands of native citizens, and that denizens should be excluded from participation as far as possible.

544. Naturalization.—The legal process by which an alien (**22**) is vested with the rights and privileges of citizenship.

2. Congress alone can pass naturalization laws.

3. Under the Articles of Confederation, the States passed naturalization laws.

4. A naturalized citizen has all the rights of a native subject except that he can not become President or Vice-President.

5. The minor children of naturalized parents are citizens by law.

6. The naturalization of the husband carries with it the naturalization of the wife.

7. No alien can be compelled to naturalize.

8. Children born abroad of American parents are also American citizens.

9. Chinese can not be naturalized.

10. Indians can not be naturalized like foreigners; but sometimes a tribe has been made citizens by a special act of Congress, and by another special act these have sometimes been allowed to give up their citizenship and return to their tribal government.

11. Whole communities sometimes have been naturalized regardless of the uniform rule; as

10

in the admission of Texas and the annexation of Hawaii.

12. *Process of naturalization:* (*1*) An alien must reside five years in the United States and one year in the State or Territory where he makes application for his papers.

(*2*) He must file in a court of record at least two years before his naturalization, a sworn declaration of his intention to become a citizen.

(*3*) Finally, he must swear or affirm that he voluntarily and forever renounces all allegiance to any foreign government; that he will support the Constitution of the United States, and renounce any title of nobility he may have.

13. An alien woman marrying a citizen becomes a citizen.

14. *Exceptions.*—An alien of legal age who has served in the United States army and who has been honorably discharged, may become a citizen by merely taking the oath of allegiance, on one year's residence within the United States previous to his application.

(*2*) An alien seaman, after making a declaration, is deemed a citizen for purposes of protection, and may be naturalized after three years' service on a United States vessel.

545. Natural Rights.—Those rights to which man by nature is entitled.

2. They are the right—

(*1*) To personal security,

(*2*) To personal liberty,

(*3*) To hold private property,

(*4*) To freedom in religious opinions.

546. Naval Academy.—A school for training naval officers. Established by Congress at Annapolis, Maryland, in 1845. It provides for the same number of students as West Point, and appointments are made in the same manner (**511,**5). Applicants must be between fifteen and twenty years of age. Students receive $500 per year from admission.

547. Naval Militia.—The naval reserve forces organized under State laws; they correspond to the State Militia.

2. The naval militia, numbering (January 1st, 1898) 3,871, is organized in seventeen States.

3. Its duty is to man vessels in time of war to protect our coasts and harbors, so that the regular navy may be free to carry on war generally at sea.

548. Navy.—All the ships and men that a nation keeps armed and prepared to wage war at sea.

2. Congress may make appropriations for the navy for longer than two years—the limit for army appropriations.

3. The President is Commander-in-Chief.

4. A State can not keep a navy in time of peace without the consent of Congress.

5. Naval officers can not be removed except on sentence of a court martial.

6. Navy regulations are made by Congress.

7. *Officers and salaries* (**45**).

549. Negotiable Paper.—Commercial paper that is transferable by indorsement or delivery.

2. Such paper is made payable to bearer or to the order of some person, and in some States, as in West Virginia, it must be made payable at a certain place.

550. Neutral.—A nation that takes no part in a war waging between other nations.

551. Nisi Prius Court.—A court presided over by a single judge of a superior law court, for the trial of civil cases by jury, as distinguished from a *Court in Banc* (**239**), where questions of law are decided.

552. Nolle Prosequi (*not to wish to prosecute*).— An entry made on the record of a court denoting that the plaintiff in a civil suit, or the prosecuting attorney in a criminal suit, abandons either the whole case or a part of it.

2. It is not equivalent to an acquittal; it merely stays proceedings, and the case may be prosecuted at a future time.

553. Nominate.—To name as a candidate for an office or position.

2. The practice is regulated by custom and not by law, except locally.

3. A voter is not compelled to vote for any party candidate.

4. The object in making nominations is to simplify elections and to keep the party vote from scattering.

554. Nominee.—A person nominated or named by others for office.

555. Nominating Convention.—A convention held for the purpose of nominating candidates for office.

2. The method was introduced into our politics in 1825 and has since become general(**609**).

556. Non-Commissioned Officer.—A subordinate officer of the army not commissioned by the President or the State executive, but appointed by the Secretary of War or by a commanding officer of the army.

2. He forms the connecting link between the commanding officer and the private soldier.

557. Nonsuit.—The discontinuing of a case in court because of its being evident that, through his neglect or failure to make out his case, the plaintiff can not recover.

2. A *voluntary* nonsuit is one granted at the request of the plaintiff.

3. A *compulsory* nonsuit is one ordered by the court when the plaintiff has plainly failed to establish his case.

4. Unless ordered on the merits of the case, a nonsuit is not a bar to subsequent action.

558. North-west Territory.—The territory west of Pennsylvania, north of the Ohio River and east of the Mississippi, ceded to the United States by New York, Virginia, Massachusetts and Connecticut, all of which claimed it (**798,1**).

2. Ohio, Indiana, Illinois, Michigan and Wisconsin were organized out of it (**798,1**).

559. Notary Public.—A public officer commissioned by the Governor to take acknowledgments, affidavits, depositions, etc., within his own county.

560. Nullification.—The making an act of Congress null and void by a State, within its territory; as the Nullification Ordinance, 1832, of South Carolina, directed against the national tariff laws.

2. No State possesses the right of nullification.

561. Nuncupative Will.—A verbal will or testament (852).

2. Such a will is valid only in certain States, where, to be legal, it must be made in the presence of two or more witnesses and reduced to writing within a limited time ranging from six to sixty days, in the various States, and must usually be probated within six months.

3. Only personal property to a limited value ranging from $100 in New Hampshire to $1,000 in California, can be disposed of by nuncupative will.

4. A soldier or sailor in active duty, may anywhere legally dispose of personal property by verbal will; but to dispose of real estate, the will must be written as in the case of other persons.

562. Oath.—A solemn declaration, made with an appeal to God for the truth of what is affirmed.

563. Octroi.—A tax levied at the gates of cities in France and a few other European countries, on goods brought into them, a small part of which tax goes into the national treasury, and the remainder into the local treasury.

564. Old Glory.—A popular nickname for the United States flag.

2. In 1831, a Salem skipper or sea captain who

was about to go on a long cruise to Southern Pacific waters, was presented a handsome flag which he named "Old Glory," and the name has been applied to our flag ever since.

565. One-Man Power.—Executive power vested in one man rather than in a board or a committee; by which, responsibility is definitely located.

566. Ordeal, Trial by.—The ancient mode of determining the guilt or innocence of an accused person by throwing him securely bound, into water; when, if he sank, he was deemed innocent; if he floated, guilty. Or, the accused was required to plunge his bare arm into boiling water, or to walk blindfolded over ground strewn with hot irons; if he escaped injury in either case, he was adjudged innocent; otherwise, guilty.

2. It was practiced on the principle that Providence would protect the innocent.

567. Orders in Council.—Royal orders issued by the king of England and his Privy Council; as the famous Orders in Council of November 11, 1807, prohibiting trade between the United States and any European country under Napoleon's power.

568. Ordinance.—A local or municipal law (536).

2. The term is also applied to certain laws enacted by the colonies, and by Congress under the Confederation (198); as the famous Ordinance of 1787, for the government of the Northwest Territory (558).

569. Origin of Government.—Government had

its origin in kinship. The *patriarchal family*, in which the father was absolute monarch and ruled as king and priest, was the first form.

2. The family broadened into the *gens* or house—a clan of several families of the same stock, bearing a common name and bound by certain common religious rites, over which the principal kinsman ruled.

3. The gens or houses united into tribes, with a kinsman as chief.

4. Tribes united, and the *state*, with its king, first appeared.

570. Ostracism.—The practice of banishing from ancient Athens by popular vote, for a term of ten years, men of great political ability and influence (509-417 B. C.).

2. It required six thousand votes to ostracise a person, who was considered honored rather than disgraced.

3. The practice fell into disuse in 417 B.C. because a notably mean man was then thus honored.

571. Outlawry.—The process of proclaiming a man an outlaw and of depriving him of the benefit and protection of law.

572. Pairing.—The practice in Congress and other bodies, of members agreeing with members of opposite parties or opinions, not to vote on certain bills or on political issues for a given time.

573. Pan-American Congress.— An international conference held in Washington in 1889, in which the United States and seventeen states of Central and South America were represented. Its purpose was the adoption of arbitration for the settlement of disputes and the establishment of closer commercial relations between the countries. Nothing definite was accomplished by it.

574. Pardon.— A full release from the penalty of a violated law.

2. The President may grant reprieves or pardons for all offenses against the United States, except in cases of impeachment (**404**).

3. The President can not pardon offenses against a State.

4. The pardoning power of the State is generally vested in the Governor; sometimes, in a Board of Pardons, as in Ohio.

5. The pardoning, reprieving and commuting powers are generally vested in the same authority.

575. Pariah.—(*a*) One of the very lowest grade in India.

(*b*) One shunned and forsaken by society.

576. Parity.— Equality; as the parity of gold and silver as money standards on the basis of sixteen to one (**737**).

577. Parliament, British.— The supreme legislative body of Great Britain. It is divided into two branches, the House of Lords (**397**) and the House of Commons (**396**). Parliament has no stated time to assemble, but comes together upon the summons of the Crown.

578. Parole.— A declaration or promise made upon one's honor to do or not to do certain things; as when a prisoner of war is released upon his parole not to fight again against his captors or to return to prison again by a stated time, etc.

579. Partisan.—An over zealous adherent to a political party.

580. Passport.—A certificate issued by the government to a citizen wishing to travel in foreign countries, certifying that he is a United States citizen.

2. It is issued by the Secretary of State (**324,** (*1*): **116**) or by a member of the Consular Service.

3. Many countries require such letters of foreign travelers.

4. The United States requires them of no one.

581. Patent.—The exclusive right to manufacture, sell or use an invention.

2. The power to regulate patents is vested in Congress.

3. A patent may be granted for (*a*) an art, (*b*) a machine, (*c*) a manufacture, (*d*) a composition of matter, (*e*) any new and useful improvement on the above, (*f*) a design.

4. A patent is issued for 17 years.

5. Before 1789, States granted patents; but the power is denied them under the Constitution.

6. A patent is assignable; but the assignment must be recorded in the patent office within three months from its date.

7. Under a patent, each article must bear the words "*patented*," with the date of the patent; otherwise the patentee loses his right to protection.

8. An applicant for a patent must swear that he believes he is the original inventor of that which he desires to patent, and accompany his application with a full description of the same, with drawings in all cases admitting of the same; and in cases of composition of matter, a specimen of each ingredient used, if required to do so by the commissioner. Models are now required only in special cases.

9. The fee is $35;—$15 to accompany the application and $20 when the patent is granted.

10. If a person believes himself to be the original inventor or discoverer, he may obtain a patent in this country even though the invention or discovery has been known or used in any foreign country before his invention or discovery thereof provided it has not been before patented, or described in any printed publication in this or any foreign country before his invention or discovery thereof, for more than two years prior to his application, and not in public use or on sale in this country for more than two years prior to his application, unless the same is proved to be abandoned.

11. A person who has obtained a patent in a foreign country may also obtain a patent for the same invention in this country provided he applies for the same within seven months after filing his application in the foreign country, and provided he is otherwise entitled thereto.

12. All suits for infringements of patent rights are tried in the Federal courts.

13. An invention to be patented must not

have been in public use or on sale more than two years in this country nor described in any printed publication here or abroad, prior to the publication.

582. Patentee.—One to whom a patent is granted by the government.

583. Paternalism.—The assumption by the government of a fatherly supervision over the business and social affairs of the individual citizen.

584. Patricide.—(*a*) The murder of a father by his child.

(*b*) One who murders his father.

585. Patriot.—One who loves and serves his country.

586. Patriotism.—Love of one's own country.

587. Patronage.—The power to appoint men to office, award contracts, etc., that a public officer has by virtue of his office.

588. Peer.—(*a*) An equal.

(*b*) In England, a member of the five temporal ranks of the higher nobility; namely, duke, marquis, earl, viscount and baron, who is entitled to a seat in the House of Lords. The dignity of the peerage is hereditary.

2. Peers may be created at the pleasure of the Crown.

589. Pension.— A fixed sum of money paid to a person regularly at stated times, usually in consideration of past services.

590. Peremptory Challenge.—An objection made to a juror without being required to give a reason for making it.

2. Each party to a suit has a right to per-

emptorily challenge jurors to a certain number varying in the different States.

591. Perjury.—Knowingly stating a material matter falsely upon the trial of a case, under oath legally administered.

2. Perjury is a felony (344) punishable by imprisonment in the State prison.

592. Personal Property.—Movable property; all property except real estate.

593. Pet Banks.—The State banks in which President Jackson caused the $40,000,000 withdrawn from the Bank of the United States in 1836 to be deposited.

594. Petition.—A written request presented to Congress, or some other organized body, or to an official, praying for some special favor set forth in the document.

2. The Constitution guarantees to the people the right of petition.

595. Petit or Trial Jury.—A body of men legally selected and sworn to declare the facts in a case tried in their presence according to the law and the evidence presented to them.

2. This jury decides civil and criminal cases.

3. It sits in open court, hears the evidence of witnesses, the arguments of counsel, the instructions of the judge as to the law applicable to the case, then retires to its room and in private agrees upon its verdict.

4. It consists of 12 members except in justices' courts, where the number is six.

5. The verdict must be unanimous.

6. If it disagrees, it is dismissed, and the case must be tried again before another jury.

7. It elects one of its members as foreman.

8. If it acquits one charged with crime, he cannot be tried again; but for cause, the judge may grant a new trial in any other case.

596. Piracy.—Robbery on the high seas.

2. It is the duty of Congress to define and punish piracy.

3. Congress made the slave trade piracy in 1820.

4. Piracy is punishable by death.

597. Pivotal State.—Any State upon the result of whose vote a presidential election depends.

598. Plaintiff.— The party that brings an action (785) against another, called the defendant.

599. Plank.—The statement of a single principle in a political platform.

600. Platform.—A formal declaration of the doctrines and principles of a political party.

2. Platforms are framed and adopted by party conventions.

601. Pleadings.— The statements of facts offered by the plaintiff and defendant in support of their respective claims.

602. Plebiscite.—A vote of the whole male voting population of a country or of a community; a decree of a nation obtained by an appeal to universal suffrage.

603. Plurality Vote.—More votes than any other one candidate for the same office receives in an election.

604. Pocket Veto.—The practice on the part of the President, of not returning to Congress, with his formal veto, a bill that he does not wish to pass, and that has been presented to him within ten days (Sundays excepted)before the adjournment of Congress, thereby making it fail, without the possibility of its being passed over his veto.

2. First used by President Jackson, in 1829.

605. Police.—The civil officers of a city or town whose duty it is to preserve good order, to protect property, to prevent and deter crime, to enforce the laws and to arrest criminals.

606. Police Court.—An inferior court held in a city or town, for the trial of persons brought before it by the police, charged with minor local offenses.

607. Police Judge, Justice or Magistrate.—A judge who presides over a police court (**606**).

608. Political Committees.—The work of the political parties is, for the most part, directed by committees.

2. The *National Committee* of each party is selected by the National Convention, and consists of a member from each State and Territory. It fixes the time and place for holding the national convention, which it calls. It also collects funds for campaign expenses, distributes literature, provides for public speeches, and has supervision of the campaign in general.

3. The *State Committee*, the *Congressional Committee*, the *State Senatorial Committee*, the *County Committee*, the *Township Committee*, ect., are chosen and organized on the same general plan as the *National Committee*, with similar duties. Their names indicate their jurisdiction.

609. Political Convention.—An assembly of voters of the same political party to nominate party candidates for office, to appoint delegates to higher conventions, and to transact any other pertinent business previously set forth in the call.

2. Our system of political conventions, taking them in their regular order, beginning with the lowest, are as follows:

3. The *Primary* or *Caucus* is called by the County Executive committee where such exists. Its duties are—

(*1*) To nominate candidates for District, Township, or Ward offices.

(*2*) To select delegates to the County Convention.

(*3*) To select a District, Township or Ward Executive Committee where customary.

(*4*) To transact any other pertinent business.

4. The *County Convention* is called by the County Executive Committee. Its duties are—

(*1*) To nominate candidates for County offices.

(*2*) To nominate Delegates or Representatives to the lower house of the State Legislature.

(*3*) To select delegates to the State, the Congressional and the State Senatorial Conventions.

(*4*) To select a new County Executive Committee.

(*5*) To transact any other pertinent business.

5. The *State Senatorial Convention* is call-

ed by the State Senatorial Executive Committee of the Senatorial District. Its duties are—

(1) To nominate a candidate for the State Senate.

(2) To select a new Senatorial Executive Committee.

(3) To transact any other pertinent business.

6. The *Congressional Convention* is called by the Congressional Executive Committee of the Congressional District. It meets every two years. Its duties are—

(1) To nominate a candidate for United States Representative.

(2) To select two delegates to the National Convention every presidential year.

(3) To select a new Congressional Executive Committee.

(4) To transact any other pertinent business.

7. The *State Convention* is called by the State Executive Committee. Its duties are—

(1) To nominate candidates for 'State offices.

(2) To select four delegates-at-large to the National Convention—two for each United States Senator—every presidential year.

(3) To nominate a Presidential Elector from each Congressional District—one for each United States Representative—and two Electors-at-large—one for each United States Senator.

(4) To select a new State Executive Committee.

11

(*5*) To transact any other pertinent business.

8. The *National Convention* is called by the National Executive Committee. Its duties are—

(*1*) To nominate candidates for President and Vice-President.

(*2*) To adopt a National Platform (**600**).

(*3*) To select a new National Executive Committee.

(*a*) The National Convention is composed of two delegates (called delegates-at-large) for each United States Senator, two delegates for each United States Representative, and two delegates for each Territory and the District of Columbia—over 800 in all.

(*b*) The Populist party apportions delegates to the different States according to their party vote in the preceding presidential election.

(*c*) There are two methods of selecting delegates: in some States all of them are selected in the State convention; but in most States, the State convention selects the delegates-at-large (**268**), and the Congressional Conventions select the others.

(*d*) The Democratic party requires a two-thirds vote of all the delegates to nominate; the Republican and other parties require but a majority vote to nominate.

(*e*) The first National Convention to nominate a presidential candidate met at Baltimore in 1831; the candidate was Wm. Wirt of Maryland, who ran on the Anti-Masonic ticket.

(*f*) Previous to 1831, party caucuses of Congressmen usually nominated the candidates for President and Vice-President, and the State Legislatures usually chose the electors.

(*g*) Previous to 1804, each elector voted for two candidates for President; the candidate receiving the largest and the next largest number of votes was declared President and Vice-President respectively.

9. *Note.*—Occasionally, special conventions are called to select delegates to the higher conventions, instead of as above indicated, which is the regular manner of selecting them.

610. Political Parties.—American political parties as such were first formed at the time of the adoption of the Constitution (**297.3**).

2. There were two parties—the *loose constructionists* or Federalists, and the *strict constructionists* or Anti-Federalists.

2. In general, later parties were outgrowths and modifications of these two great systems as follows:

1. Loose Constructionists.

1. FEDERAL PARTY.—1887-1816. One of the two original parties.

2. *Principal Leaders.*—Hamilton, Washington and John Adams.

3. *Principles.*—(*a*) Favored a strong central government.

(*b*) Favored loose construction of the Constitution (**297**).

(c) Opposed aiding France in her Revolution.

(*d*) Opposed the purchase of Louisiana.

(e) Opposed the War of 1812.

(f) Favored a United States Bank.

(2) *Presidents.*—George Washington, 1789-1797, and John Adams, 1797-1801.

(3) Opposition to the War of 1812 was the main cause of its extinction.

2. NATIONAL REPUBLICAN PARTY.—1824-1834. It grew out of the *Federal* party.

(1) *Principles.*—It favored:

(a) Loose construction.

(b) A United States Bank.

(c) A Protective Tariff.

(d) Internal improvements.

(2) *Leaders.*—Daniel Webster, Henry Clay and J. Q. Adams.

(3) *President.*—J. Q. Adams, 1825-1829.

3. WHIG PARTY.—1834-1852. Another name for the National Republican party reinforced by the Anti-Masonic party and the Nullifiers and States'-rights men of the South.

(1) *Principles.*—(a) Same as those held by the National Republican party. Also—

(b) Opposed the annexation of Texas.

(c) Opposed the Mexican War.

(d) Favored limited veto power.

(e) Favored the Compromise of 1850.

(2) *Leaders.*—Webster, Clay and J. Q. Adams, who were the leaders of the National Republican party.

(3) *Presidents.*—Wm. Henry Harrison and Tyler, 1841-1845. Taylor and Fillmore, 1849-1853.

Note.—The term *Whig* was also applied to the colonists that opposed Great Britain and favored the Revolutionary War, as opposed to the *Tories*, who favored Great Britain and opposed the War.

4. REPUBLICAN PARTY.—1856-**. Formed by . the union of the Whigs, the Free Soilers, many Know-Nothings and a few Democrats.

(a) The name was formally adopted by a Michigan convention in 1854; the first national convention was held in 1856.

(1) *Principles.*—The party stands for:

(a) National Banks.

(b) Protective tariff and reciprocity.

(c) A Gold standard.

(d) Many things held in common with the Democratic party.

(2) *Presidents.*—Lincoln and Johnson, 1861-69; Grant, 1869-77; Hayes, 1877-81; Garfield, and Arthur, 1881-85; Benj. Harrison, 1889-93; McKinley, 1897—.

2. Strict Constructionists.

1. ANTI-FEDERALIST PARTY.—1787-1792. One of the two original parties.

(1) *Principles.*—It stood:

(a) For strict construction of the Constitution.

(b) Opposed to a strong central government.

(c) Opposed to the United States Bank.

(2) *Leaders.*—Jefferson, Madison, Monroe, and Gerry.

2. DEMOCRATIC-REPUBLICAN PARTY.—1792-1824. The Anti-Federal party, joined by the Republicans and Democrats—offshoots of the Federal party.

(1) Principles.—(*a*) It advocated the principles held by the Anti-Federalists above, and in addition, it—

(*b*) Favored the War of 1812.

(*c*) Favored the purchase of Louisiana.

(2) Leaders.—Jefferson, Madison and Randolph.

(3) Presidents.—Jefferson, 1801-9; Madison, 1809-17; Monroe, 1817-25.

3. DEMOCRATIC PARTY.—1824-**. An outgrowth of the Democratic-Republican party.

(1) Principles.—It stands:

(*a*) Against the issuing of national bank notes by the national banks.

(*b*) For the free coinage (**368**) of silver at the ratio of 16 to 1.

(*c*) For a revenue tariff.

(*d*) For many things in common with the Republican party.

(2) Presidents.—Jackson, 1829-37; Van Buren, 1837-41; Polk, 1845-49; Pierce, 1853-57; Buchanan, 1857-61; Cleveland, 1885-89 and 1893-97.

3. Minor Political Parties.

1. ANTI-MASONIC PARTY.—1827-36. It sprang chiefly from the National Republican party after the Morgan episode of 1826.

(1) It opposed the Masonic and all other secret orders.

(2) In 1831, it nominated William Wirt for President, and Amos Ellmaker for Vice-President. They received the electoral vote of Vermont.

(3) In 1835, it elected a governor in Pennsylvania.

(*4*) It finally merged into the Whig party.

2. ABOLITION OR LIBERTY PARTY.—1840-48. It sprang chiefly from the Whig party.

(*1*) It stood for the abolition of slavery.

(*2*) It defeated Clay in 1844 by nominating its own presidential candidate.

(*3*) It joined the Barn-burners and northern Whigs to form the Free Soil party.

3. FREE SOIL PARTY.—1848-56. Made up of Abolitionists, Barn-burners and northern Whigs.

(*1*) It stood for "A free soil to a free people;" it opposed the extension of slavery, the Fugitive Slave Act, and the Compromise of 1850, and favored international arbitration.

(*2*) Charles Sumner, Salmon P. Chase, Wm. H. Seward and John Hall were the principal leaders.

(*3*) It joined the Whigs and other minor factions to form the Republican party.

4. AMERICAN OR KNOW-NOTHING PARTY.— 1852-59. It had its origin in a secret organization called *"The Sons of '76,"* or *"The Order of the Star-Spangled Banner,"* whose members were sworn to answer "I don't know" to questions relating to the society; hence its name.

(*1*) It opposed the naturalization of aliens until they had been residents here twenty-one years. Its principle was "Americans must rule America."

(*2*) Millard Fillmore was its chief leader.

5. CONSTITUTIONAL UNION PARTY.—1860. A re-organization of the Know-Nothing party

(*1*) It held for "the Constitution of the country, the union of the States, and the enforcement of the laws."

(*2*) In 1860, the leaders, John Bell and Edward Everett, were nominated for President and Vice-President respectively, and received thirty nine electoral votes.

(*3*) Its membership was absorbed by the Democratic and Republican parties soon after the campaign of 1860.

6. NATIONAL OR GREENBACK PARTY.—1876-88. It was composed of members from the Democratic and Republican parties.

(*1*) It favored an unlimited issue of greenback currency, and an income tax; it opposed monopolies.

(*2*) Benjamin F. Butler and James B. Weaver were its principal leaders.

(*3*) When it dissolved, most of its members went to the Populist or People's party.

7. PROHIBITION PARTY.—1869-**. It came chiefly from the Republican party.

(*1*) It opposes the manufacture and sale of intoxicating liquors, and favors woman suffrage and free trade.

(*2*) Neale Dow and John P. St. John were among its principal leaders.

8. POPULIST OR PEOPLE'S PARTY.—1891-**. It is made up of members from all other parties, but is chiefly a union of all agricultural and labor organizations.

(*1*) It stands for free silver at 16 to 1, an income tax, government ownership of railroads and telegraphs, the initiative (**422**) and referendum (**677**), postal savings banks; and opposes national banks.

(*2*) *Leaders*, James B. Weaver and Jeremiah Simpson.

9. BARN-BURNERS.—1844-48. In 1844, the election of Polk split the Democratic party in New York, into two factions; the Barn-burners being one of them: the other being the Hunkers.

(*1*) They favored Van Buren and opposed the extension of slavery.

(*2*) They helped form the Free Soil party in 1848.

(*3*) They took their name from the story applied to them on account of their radical measures, of the man who burned his barn to free it from rats.

10. HUNKERS.—1844-60. (*See 9 above*).

(*1*) They supported Polk's administration and favored the extension of slavery. The faction ceased to exist just before the Civil War.

11. ANTI-RENTERS.—1840-50. A party in New York that opposed the collection of back rents by the son of Stephen Van Rensselaer who died in 1839.

(*1*) They overpowered the militia sent against them (the "Helderberg War") and for a time held the balance of power in New York politics.

(*2*) In 1850, the owners of the manors (**496**) sold the land to the tenants, and the anti-rent movement ceased.

12. LOCO-FOCOS.—1835-37. First called the

Equal Rights Party. A Democratic faction in New York, that organized to oppose State banks because the Legislature *sold charters.*

(*1*) In an Equal Rights meeting in 1835, some regular Democrats attended and attempted to direct the proceedings. They failed, and blew out the lights. The Equal Rights men lit *loco-foco* matches and proceeded with the business. Thenceforward, they were known as Loco-Focos.

(*2*) They finally returned to their party.

13. CONSERVATIVES.—1837-40. The Democrats that voted with the Whigs against the subtreasury bill, which was supported by the regular Democratic party.

14. STALWARTS.—Those Republicans who stood boldly and firmly in the national convention of 1880 for Grant's election to the presidency a third time.

(*1*) They were led by Roscoe Conkling.

(*2*) Their opponents were the *Half-breeds,* who were led by James G. Blaine.

(*3*) The death of Garfield and the accession of Arthur, a Stalwart, healed the disorder.

15. CLINTONIANS and BUCKTAILS.—1812-1828. The two factions of the Democratic-Republican party in New York during the time indicated.

(*1*) The *Clintonians* favored Governor De Witt Clinton's canal policy and supported him for President in 1812.

(*2*) The *Bucktails* stood by Madison and opposed Clinton's canal policy throughout.

(*3*) The death of Clinton in 1828 ended the

factions.

16. DOUGHFACES.—The eighteen northern members of Congress who voted for the Missouri Compromise in 1820; applied to them by John Randolph, of Roanoke.

(*1*) Later, it was generally applied to northerners who favored slavery, or who appeared to be too anxious to please the South.

17. SILVER GRAYS, CONSCIENCE WHIGS OR SNUFF TAKERS.—The Whigs that consciencionsly opposed the extension of slavery in the 50's.

(*1*) Those who favored such extension for the sake of holding the southern Whigs, were called *Cotton Whigs, Woolly Heads, or Seward Whigs*.

18. LIBERAL REPUBLICANS.—1870-72. A faction of the Republican party dissatisfied with Grant's first term, that joined the Democrats in the support of Horace Greeley for President.

19. EQUAL RIGHTS PARTY.—(*See Loco-Focos.*) Belva A. Lockwood's party, which she organized in 1884, and in which she nominated herself for President. She advocated equal rights and suffrage for women.

20. UNION LABOR PARTY.—A national organization formed in 1887. It held the same principles as the present People's party, which absorbed it in 1891.

2. There have been various other labor organizations of minor importance.

21. AMERICAN PARTIES.—There have been various American parties under different

names, discriminating against foreigners.

611. Political Right.—The right to vote and to take part in the conduct of public affairs.

612. Political Ring.—A number of men combined to control political affairs to their own interest, to the exclusion of all others; as the famous Tweed Ring of New York (**822**).

613. Politician.—One who engages in politics as a business, usually for his own advantage.

614. Politics.—The science and management of government.

615. Poll Book.—A register of persons qualified to vote at an election. A book containing the poll list.

616. Poll List.—A list of persons voting at the polls.

617. Polls or Polling Place.—The place where votes are cast in an election.

618. Poll Tax.—A tax levied upon the polls or heads, of male citizens between certain ages varying in the different States.

2. In some States where women vote such women also pay poll tax.

3. The payment of poll tax is a qualification for voting in several States.

619. Polygamy.—The having of two or more wives or husbands at the same time.

620. Popular Vote.—The vote cast at the polls by the whole body of voters.

621. Port.—A harbor where vessels receive and unload their cargoes.

2. A *port of entry* is where duties are collected; as New York, New Orleans and San

Francisco.

3. To *enter* a port is to report a vessel with her cargo at the customhouse, with a statement of imported goods, for the purpose of paying duties and obtaining permission to land the cargo.

4. To *clear* from a port is to obtain from the customhouse officers the necessary papers to sail.

622. Portfolio.—The office and functions of a member of the cabinet or minister of State.

623. Postal Service.—The postal service is under the direct control of Congress, as it is in all civilized nations.

(*2*) The Postmaster General has general supervision. He has three Assistant Postmasters General. He appoints all postmasters receiving less than $1000; the President appoints the others.

(*3*) Before 1845, postage on letters varied from six cents to twenty-five cents according to distance and was paid by the receiver. At that date, it was reduced to from five to ten cents.

(*4*) There are over 75,000 post offices in this country.

(*5*) There are four classes of mail matter—

(*1*) *First class*, written or sealed matter, two cents per ounce or fraction thereof.

(*2*) *Second class*, regular publications, one cent per four ounces.

(*3*) *Third class*, all other printed matter, one cent per two ounces.

(*4*) *Fourth class*, merchandise, one cent per

ounce.

5. Within the Postal Union (**829**), letters are carried for five cents each per half ounce, and postal cards for two cents.

6. There were some crude postal arrangements in this country as early as 1692.

7. Stamps were introduced here in 1847; registration, in 1855 ; postal money orders, in 1864.

624. Postal Treaty.—A treaty between different nations, providing for the mutual transmission and delivery of mail matter.

3. On the part of the United States, the Postmaster General, with the consent of the President, makes such treaties, and when thus made, they do not require the ratification of the Senate as do other treaties.

625. Power of Attorney.—Written authority given by one person to another to transact business for him.

626. Powers of Congress.—*Constitution I., 8.*

627. Powers of States.—States may pass any laws not forbidden by their constitutions or by the Constitution of the United States, and all such laws are binding until repealed or declared by the courts to be unconstitutional.

628. Preamble.—The introductory part of a constitution or statute (**769**), which sets forth the reasons and purposes for which it is framed.

629. Preemption Law.—A law passed (the present law) in 1841 giving any citizen 21 years old 160 acres of public land at the end of a year for settling on the same, building a house, and paying $1.25 or $2.50 per acre according to location.

630. Presentment.—An accusation made by a grand jury (383) against a person, from their own knowledge or observation, or from evidence before them, without having a bill of indictment (82) presented to them.

2. When a presentment is made, the prosecuting officer must frame a bill of indictment, and the accused be formally indicted (415), before he can be tried.

631. President.—The chief executive officer of an organized body of individuals or society.

632. Presidential Offices.—Postoffices paying a salary of $1,000 or more, and whose postmasters are appointed by the President.

633. President's Flag.—A special flag displayed by any vessel carrying the President. It was first suggested by President Arthur in 1882 and first used by him in 1883.

634. President's Message.—A message sent by a President to Congress at the opening of each session, to be read to each house by its Clerk, and which contains information of the state of the Union, and recommends such measures as the President deems necessary and expedient, as provided by the Constitution.

2. The message is accompanied by official documents and the full reports of the various departments of government.

3. Washington and John Adams delivered their messages in each case orally to both houses assembled in the Senate Chamber, and

in each case each house appointed a committee to formulate a reply, which when adopted was sent to the President.

4. Jefferson wrote his message and sent it to Congress (1801). Since then this method has prevailed, and the practice of replying to the President's message was discontinued at that time.

5. Congress is not required to follow the recommendations set forth in the President's message—a distinctive feature of our government.

6. The President sends special messages to Congress when he deems it necessary.

635. President's Oath.—The oath required to be taken by the President-elect before entering upon the duties of his office. It is as follows:

2. "I do solemnly swear (or affirm) that I will faithfully execute the office of President of the United States, and will, to the best of my ability, preserve, protect and defend the Constitution of the United States."

636. President, U. S.—The chief executive officer of our government.

2. He is nominated by the National Convention of his party, and is elected by the Presidential Electors (**302**).

3. If the Electors fail to elect a President, the House of Representatives does so (**398**).

4. His term of office is four years.

5. His salary is $50,000 per year. It can neither be increased nor decreased during his term of office, and is payable monthly out of

the National Treasury.

6. He can receive no presents from any foreign government, from the United States nor from any State, but may do so from private individuals (376).

7. He must be (*a*) a natural-born citizen, (*b*) at least 35 years of age, and (*c*) must have been a resident of the United States 14 years.

8. He can not interfere with Congress except through his veto (835) power.

9. His veto power, and his power to make treaties are the *legislative* powers of the President (636.9).

10. He is Commander-in-Chief of the United States Army and Navy, and of the militia of the several States, when called into the actual service of the United States.

11. "He shall take care that the laws are faithfully executed."

12. He may grant reprieves (687) and pardons (574) for all offenses against the United States, except in cases of impeachment (404).

13. He may require the written opinions of his Cabinet (116) officers on any questions relating to their respective departments (324).

14. He may make treaties (817) with foreign nations, subject to ratification by two-thirds of the Senate.

15. He may call, at will, special sessions of Congress, or of either house.

16. He receives Ambassadors and Ministers from other countries.

17. With the consent of the Senate, he ap-

points Ambassadors, (27), other public ministers (516), Consuls (218), Judges of the Supreme Court (787), his Cabinet, Customs officers (171), Postmasters who receive $1,000 per year or more, and all other Federal officers whose appointments are not otherwise provided for.

18. The Constitution makes all his appointments subject to ratification by the Senate, but empowers Congress to provide by law for the appointment of such inferior officers as it thinks proper, by the President alone, by courts of law, or by heads of departments, without such ratification. A great majority of the appointments are now thus made.

19. He fills vacancies in office occurring when the Senate is not in session; but commissions (183) to fill such vacancies expire at the close of the next session of the Senate.

20. He can adjourn Congress when it can not decide on a time for adjournment; but this power has never been exercised.

21 A Presidential appointment is made as follows:

(a) The President nominates in writing.

(b) The Senate votes to confirm.

(c) The President appoints.

(d) A commission is issued bearing the signature of the President and the seal of the U.S.

22. He can'at will remove officers appointed by him.

23. It is his duty to keep Congress informed on the condition of the Union and to recommend such measures as he shall deem necessa-

ry and expedient. This he does in his message
(634).

24. The President must take the following
oath or affirmation: "I do solemnly swear
(or affirm) that I will faithfully execute the
office of President of the United States, and
will, to the best of my ability, preserve, protect and defend the Constitution of the United
States."

25. The Chief Justice of the Supreme Court
administers the oath to the President.

26. His term of office begins at 12 o'clock M.
on the fourth day of March, at which time he
is inaugurated immediately after the inauguration of the Vice-President (836).

27. By the Presidential Succession Law of
1886, in case of the death, removal or resignation of both the President and Vice-President,
the office of the President is filled in the following order of succession:—

(1) By the Secretary of State.

(2) By the Secretary of the Treasury.

(3) By the Secretary of War.

(4) By the Attorney General.

(5) By the Postmaster General.

(6) By the Secretary of the Navy.

(7) By the Secretary of the Interior.

(a) The Secretary of Agriculture was not at
that time (1886), a Cabinet Officer.

637. Previous Question.—The question
whether or not debate shall cease and a vote
be taken at once on a motion already before
an assembly.

2. A member moves "The previous question,"

and the presiding officer asks: "Shall the main question be now put?"

3. If this question carries, debate ceases at once; further amendments are out of order, and the subject under consideration must be voted upon immediately.

4. If the question fails, the business proceeds as if the previous question had not been moved.

638. Primary.—A caucus (133); a district, township or ward mass meeting of the voters of the same political party, to nominate candidates to fill local offices, to select delegates to the county convention, ect.

639. Primary Election.—The method of selecting party candidates and delegates instead of in a convention.

2. The election is held on the same day throughout the given territory, and only those may vote who are legal voters of the party holding the election.

640. Privateer.—A private vessel carrying letters of marque and reprisal (475).

641. Prize, or Prize of War.—A ship or goods of an enemy captured at sea in time of war.

2. When a prize is lawfully captured, it is taken to the nearest court, condemned and sold at auction, and the net proceeds are divided by the court according to law.

3. When a vessel captures a prize equal or superior to itself, the entire prize is decreed to the captors, to be divided according to rank; but when it captures a prize inferior to itself, one half goes to the United States and the other half is divided among the captors as indi-

cated.

4. In the case of privateers, the entire prize goes to the captors.

5. To be a lawful prize, a vessel must be taken on the high seas, or on the territorial seas of the belligerents. No prize can be lawfully taken on neutral waters.

6. With the exception of contraband goods, neutral goods on the enemy's vessel or the enemy's goods on a neutral vessel, can not be taken as a prize of war.

642. Prize Court.—A court that decides whether a ship taken at sea during war, has been lawfully captured as a prize of war; and if so, it condemns it, and apportions it according to United States laws.

2. In this country, the United States District Court sits as a prize court, where questions as to prizes are settled, with an appeal lying to the United States Supreme Court.

643. Prize Money.—The part of the net proceeds of a prize of war that is paid to the officers and crew of a man-of-war as a reward for making the capture.

644. Proclamation.—An official public announcement.

645. Prohibitions upon the States.—(870).

646. Prohibitions upon the United States.—(869).

647. Promissory Note.—A written promise to pay a certain sum of money to a certain specified party at a certain future time.

2. The *maker* is the party that signs the note.

3. The *payee* is the party named in the note, to be paid.

648. Proscription.—The act practiced by the Romans, of dooming to death, exile or outlawry, by posting in public a list of the names of those proscribed.

649. Prosecuting Attorney.—The public lawyer who prosecutes criminals and gives legal advice to county officers.

650. Protection.—The theory that home producers should be protected against foreign competition in their own markets, by imposing a protective tariff (**790**) on imports (**407**).

651. Protectionist.—One who believes in the theory of protection (**650**).

652. Pro tempore.—For the time; as chairman *pro tempore*, etc.

653. Protest.—A formal written declaration made by a notary public, of the non-payment of a note or other negotiable paper when due, and protesting against all who are liable for its payment.

654. Protocol.—The original or rough draft of a treaty or other writing.

655. Proxy.—(*a*) A person who votes or acts for another as his substitute.

(*b*) The writing by which one person is authorized to vote or act for another.

656. Public Debt.—The public debt is in three forms: (*a*) bonds (**97**), (*b*) floating debt (**352**), and (*c*) treasury notes or "greenbacks" (**384**).

657. Qualify.—To take the required oath of office before assuming official duties.

658. Quarantine.—The cutting off of a place on account of malignant contagious disease therein, from all intercourse with the outside world.

2. By the laws of Congress, all vessels are subject to the laws of the State at whose ports they arrive.

659. Quartering Soldiers.—Furnishing them with board and lodging.

660. Quartermaster.—An army officer who provides quarters, clothing, horses and other necessary supplies for the soldiers.

661. Quash.—To annul; to make void; as to quash an indictment (**415**).

662. Quorum.—The number of members of a body required to be present before business can be transacted.

2. In each house of Congress, and in all State Legislatures, a majority of the members elected constitutes a quorum.

3. But fewer than a quorum can—

(*a*) Adjourn from day to day, and

(*b*) Compel absent members to attend.

4. In the election of a Vice-President by the Senate (**724**), however, two-thirds of the whole number of Senators constitute a quorum; and in the election of a President by the House (**399**), a representation of one or more members from two-thirds of all the States, constitutes a quorum.

663. Quo Warranto.—A writ issuing from a court of law, requiring a person or body of persons to show by what warrant, right or authority they hold or exercise a franchise or privilege, or hold public office.

664. Radicals.—Those who advocate positive change in matters of government.

665. Railroading.—The rushing a bill through a legislative assembly by the efforts of corrupt members.

666. Ratify.—To establish, or to make something valid by giving sanction to it.

667. Real Estate or Property.—Lands and the buildings thereon.

668. Rebellion.—Open and avowed forcible resistance to, and renunciation of, the authority of a government, with a view to overthrow it.

669. Reciprocity.—A mutual agreement between two nations to confer equal privileges upon each other in regard to customs duties, etc.

2. The United States has reciprocity treaties with several governments.

670. Recognizance.—An obligation having the effect of a bail bond, but differing from it in that it is made orally and sworn to in open court and noted on its records.

671. Reconstruction.—The reorganizing, after the Civil War, of the eleven seceded States, and the bringing them back into the Union, with their former constitutional rights.

2. Tennessee was the first State restored, July 24, 1866; and Georgia the last, July 15, 1870.

672. Reconstruction Committee.—A committee of 15 appointed by Congress December, 1865, to inquire into the condition of the seceded States and to report in regard to reconstruction (**671**).   ·

2. The appointment of this committee greatly displeased President Johnson, and hastened the open disturbance between him and Congress.

673. Red Cross Society.—An international association organized for the relief of the sick and the wounded in war.

2. It was organized at the Geneva Convention, an international congress called for that purpose at Geneva, Switzerland, in 1864.

3. By the international treaty arranged at that convention, ambulances, military hospitals and all persons attached thereto, are protected and made neutral.

4. The distinctive flag and arm-badge of the association have a red cross on a white ground—the Geneva cross.

674. Red Tape.—Extreme and unnecessary official formality exercised in the transaction of public business.

675. Reeve.—An officer; as governor, steward, etc. In early times, an English magistrate. Now used only in compounds, as shire-reeve, or sheriff.

676. Referee.—A person to whom a question in dispute is referred for decision.

677. Referendum.—The practice of submitting important legislative acts to a vote of the people for ratification before they can become law. It is practiced in Switzerland.

2. It is practiced indirectly in the United States by embodying in the State Constitution, non-constitutional provisions, or mat_

ters properly belonging to statute law.

3. In Minnesota and Wisconsin, a few certain laws depend directly upon the vote of the people for their validity.

678. Refunding.—The replacing of existing bonds with new bonds, usually for the purpose of securing a lower rate of interest.

679. Regents.—A board of directors or trustees; usually of a college or university.

680. Regicide.—One who murders a king.

681. Registration.—The method adopted in some States, especially in large cities, of preventing illegal voting by requiring citizens to satisfy the registration officers some days before the election that such citizens are legal voters, and to have their names enrolled on a register of those only who may vote.

682. Regulars.—Soldiers belonging to the standing army (**44,2**).

683. Remonetization.—The act of restoring anything as current money or legal tender; as the remonetization of silver in 1873.

684. Repeater.—A person who votes at different polls during the same election.

685. Replevin.—An action brought to recover one's personal property wrongfully held by another.

686. Representative, U. S.—A member of the lower house of Congress.

2. There are 357, or one for every 173,901 inhabitants.

3. They are elected every even year, each Congressional District electing one.

4. The term of office is two years, beginning

March 4th next succeeding the election.

5. Representatives receive $5,000 per year and 20 cents per mile in going to and returning from a session of Congress.

6. The Speaker of the House receives $8,000 per year.

7. Representatives are paid monthly out of the national treasury.

8. A Representative must be—

(*a*) 25 years of age.

(*b*) Seven years a citizen of the United States.

(*c*) A resident of the State in which he is elected, at the time of his election.

9. He need not necessarily be a voter: he may have just moved into the State.

10. He may move from the State after his election and still serve out his term.

11. He need not necessarily be a resident of the Congressional District electing him.

12. He is the only Federal officer elected by popular vote.

13. Those who may legally vote for members of the lower house of a State Legislature, may vote for United States Representatives.

14. Each State must have at least one Representative.

15. A person can hold no other Federal office while he is a Representative.

16. He can not, during the time for which he was elected, be appointed to any civil Federal office created, or the salary of which has been increased, during such time. But he may be appointed to such a *military* office at

any time, or to such a *civil* office after the term for which he was elected has expired.

17. Representatives must be elected in districts of contiguous territory, by written or printed ballots, and on the same day throughout the United States (the first Tuesday after the first Monday in November), except where State Constitutions prescribe a different day.

18. The Constitution does not limit the number of Representatives except that the representation must not exceed one for every 30,000 inhabitants.

19. Representatives represent the *people*, while Senators represent the *State*.

20. Representatives are sworn in by the Speaker, who is himself sworn in by the Father of the House.

687. Reprieve.—The suspension for a time of the execution of a sentence; as to postpone the execution of a criminal.

688. Repudiation.—The act of renouncing or of disclaiming anything; as to repudiate a debt, etc.

2. A State may repudiate its own contracts, in which case no court can enforce them, as no State can be sued.

3. But no State can pass laws impairing the obligation of lawful contracts between individuals, which would be unconstitutional.

689. Requisition.—A formal demand made by the authorities of one State or country upon those of another, for the surrender of a fugitive criminal (**335**).

690. Resignation.—The formal surrender of an office.

(*a*) An elective officer usually addresses his resignation to the officer authorized to fill the vacancy or to order a new election, and (*b*) an appointive officer usually sends his resignation to the authority that appointed him.

691. Resolution.—A formal expression of purpose, determination, opinion or principle, presented to a deliberative body for discussion and adoption by vote.

2. A *simple resolution* is one passed by a single house, whose affairs alone it affects.

3. A *concurrent resolution* is one passed concurrently by the House and Senate, but not intended to have the force of law.

4. A *joint resolution* is one passed concurrently by both houses and intended to have the force of law—a temporary law, usually.

(*a*) A joint resolution must be read three times before its passage, and requires the signature of the President to make it valid; any other resolution is read but once, and does not require the President's signature.

692. Respite.—A reprieve (**687**).

693. Retroactive Law.—A law that affects acts done prior to the enactment of the law.

2. In criminal matters, such a law is forbidden; but in civil matters, such a law, of a curative nature, may be passed.

694. Returning Boards.—Boards provided for by the reconstructed States of the South generally; usually composed of three State officers and two citizens, and empowered to canvass the votes and declare the results of all elections.

2. The object was to guard against intimidation in elections by disfranchised (285) citizens.

695. Revenue.—The money collected by the government for public purposes. The income of the government.

2. The national revenue is practically all raised by indirect taxation (792,3), from customs duties (296) and excise duties (321).

3. All bills for raising national revenue must originate in the House; but the Senate may propose amendments.

4. Congress enacts all national revenue laws (695).

5. State revenue is raised mainly by direct taxation (792,4).

696. Revenue Bill.—A bill to *raise* money for the support of the government.

2. Such a bill must originate in the House of Representatives.

3. But the Senate may originate bills *appropriating* money.

697. Revenue Cutter.—A small, fleet vessel employed by the government at ports of entry (621,2) to aid in enforcing the revenue laws.

698. Revolt.—A renunciation of allegiance to a government with a view to overthrow or to change it by force.

699. Revolution.—A fundamental change in the political organization of a government, brought about by rebellion.

700. Rider.—A special additional clause, usually containing an unpopular feature, annexed to an already complete bill, in the course of legislation, in order that it may ride through on the popularity of the main bill.

701. Righ of Suffrage.—The right to vote.

702. Riot.—A tumultuous disturbance of the public peace, by three or more persons unlawfully assembled, for the execution by violence, of some private purpose either lawful or unlawful.

703. Robbery.—The forcible and unlawful taking of goods of another in his presence against his will, or by putting him in fear of bodily injury.

2. It is made a felony by statute.

704. Roorbach.—A falsehood or ficticious story published for political intrigue. The term originated in the campaign of 1844.

705. Rotation in Office.—The practice of frequently changing public officers by dismissing them and substituting new men.

706. Round Robin.—A written petition, protest, remonstrance, or memorial, with the names of the signers written in a circle so that no name appears first on the list, thus designating no parties as leaders.

707. Royalty.—The percentage, or the share of profit paid by a publisher or manufacturer, to the owner of a copyright or patent, for the right to issue the publication, or to manufacture the article.

708. Salary Grab.—A term applied to an act of Congress of March 3, 1873, paying Senators and Representatives $7,500 per year, and the Speaker of the House, $10,000, with back pay (Act March 4, 1873) from March 4, 1871.

2. The act also raised without back pay, the salary of the President to $50,000; of the Chief Justice, to $10,500; those of the Vice-President, the Cabinet officers and the Associate Justices, to $10,000.

3. The next Congress repealed the laws except as they affected the salaries of the President and Justices.

709. Salute.—A mark of respect shown by firing guns, dipping flags, etc.

2. The Salute to the Union consists in firing a gun for every State in the Union. It is fired every Fourth of July, at noon, at every military post and on board United States naval vessels.

3. The National Salute, to the national flag, the President and royal personages; twenty one guns.

4. The salute to the flag is the only salute returned, which must be done within 24 hours.

5. Other salutes are: for Vice-President, 19 guns; for Cabinet officers, Governors of States, commanding Generals and Admirals, 17 guns; for United States and foreign Ambassadors, 15 guns; and for Major Generals, 13 guns, etc.

6. All salutes are fired between sunrise and sunset.

710. Salvage.—That part of the property or value thereof, allowed to the owner, master and crew of a vessel that voluntarily saves another vessel or her cargo when abandoned or in great peril at sea.

2. It sometimes amounts to one-half the value of the property saved.

3. Its object is to encourage vessels to aid each other when in danger.

711. Scratching.—Erasing or canceling the name or names of candidates from a ballot, thereby refusing to vote for some of the party candidates.

712. Seal.—A formally adopted device engraved on a stamp for officially stamping documents as evidence of their authenticity.

2. A *Great Seal* is the principal seal of a State or of a nation.

3. The Secretary of State is the custodian of the Great Seal of the United States. He affixes it to all executive documents, commissions and important State papers.

4. The *Lesser Seal* is used in some of the States for stamping unimportant documents.

5. The United States has no lesser seal.

713. Sealed Orders.—Orders sealed and delivered to a commander in the Navy, to be opened only after his vessel has put to sea or has reached a certain designated point.

714. Sea Letter.—The passport (580) which a neutral merchant vessel must carry in time of war.

715. Search Warrant.—A warrant legally authorizing an officer to search a certain house or place for stolen goods (888).

716. Secession.—The voluntary withdrawal of a State or States from the National Union.

13

2. Eleven States seceded in 1860 and 1861.

3. The first suggestion of secession was made by Josiah Quincy, of Massachusetts, in 1811, who said in Congress, that if Louisiana should be admitted into the Union as a State, "It will be the right of all and the duty of some [States] definitely to prepare for separation; amicably if they can, violently if they must."

717. Secession Ordinance.—An act passed by the Legislature of a State, declaring for secession (**716**).

2. Secession ordinances were passed by the eleven seceding States in 1860-61.

718. Secretary of Legation.—The secretary of an embassy or legation (**308**).

2. He usually temporarily assumes the duties of the Minister in case of his removal.

719. Sedition.—The raising of a feeling of discontent and opposition in a State, without intending open violence against the laws.

720. Seigniorage.—The difference between the actual cost of a quantity of bullion and the face value of the coin made from it.

2. The seigniorage is turned into the national treasury and belongs to the government.

721. Selectmen.—The trustees or board of officers of the New England town, who transact the public business.

722. Senate.—The upper, less numerous, and more distinguished branch of Congress or of a State Legislature.

723. Senate Chamber.—The hall in which a Senate meets to transact business.

724. Senate, United States.—The upper and

less numerous house of Congress.

2. It is composed (1899) of ninety members—two from each State.

3. It has the sole power to try impeachments (**404**).

4. It ratifies treaties (**817**) and confirms appointments made by the President (**636**).

5. It is a continuous body, and is always organized and ready for business immediately upon convening.

6. It represents the *Federal* idea of our government—the States—while the House of Representatives represents the *National* idea —the people.

7. It makes its own rules of procedure.

8. It elects its committees by ballot; while in the House, they are appointed by the Speaker.

9. The Vice-President of the United States is *ex officio* (**329**) President of the Senate; but he can not vote except in case of a tie.

10. It elects a President *pro tempore* (**652**) to preside over the Senate in the absence of the Vice-President.

11. The President may call it into extra executive session without calling the House.

12. It may punish its members for disorderly behavior in any way it deems proper (**201, 22**).

13. It may expel a member by a two-thirds quorum vote (**662**).

14. It elects a Vice-President of the United States if the Electors fail to do so (**836**).

15. The length of speeches is not limited in

the Senate as in the House.

16. The yea and nay vote (859) must be recorded in the journal if one-fifth of the members present demand it.

17. The Senate is judge of the election, returns and qualifications of its own members.

18. The first Senate opened with nineteen members.

19. The Chief Justice presides when the President is impeached (404).

20. The oath of office is administered by the Vice-President.

21. It elects the following officers:

(1) A President *pro tempore* to preside in the absence of the Vice-President.

(2) A Chief Clerk.

(3) A Sergeant-at-Arms.

(4) A Postmaster.

(5) A Librarian.

(6) A Chaplain.

(7) A Doorkeeper, and a very large number of subordinates, none of whom are Senators except the President *pro tempore*.

22. The presiding officer is addressed as "Mr. President."

23. It can not adjourn for more than three days at a time, nor to any other place than that in which it is sitting, without the consent of the House.

24. If vacancies occur in appointive Federal offices when the Senate is not in session, the President may fill the same temporarily until the Senate meets.

25. When a vacancy occurs in the Senate,

the Legislature of the State from which the vacancy occurs, on the *second* *Tuesday* after notice of such vacancy is received, proceeds to elect a Senator for the unexpired term.

26. If such State Legislature is not in session when such vacancy occurs, the Governor appoints a Senator to serve until the Legislature convenes and elects one.

27. The Senate has concurrent jurisdiction with the House in enacting laws.

28. Each daily session of the Senate is opened with prayer.

29. Senators and Representatives are not Federal officers, and cannot be impeached.

House of Representatives, (399); *Congress,* (201); *Representatives,* (686).

725. Senator, U. S.—A member of the upper house of Congress.

2. There are 90 Senators—two from each State.

3. Senators represent the *States,* while Representatives represent the *people.*

4. Congress may by law regulate the election of Senators, except as to the places of choosing them.

5. The first Federal law governing the election of Senators was passed in 1866, when the present mode of election was provided.

6. In 1789, the Senators were divided by lot into three classes; one-third of them retiring every two years, thus making the Senate practically a perpetual body.

7. The term of a Senator is six years.

8. He (a) must be thirty years old.

(*b*) Must have been a citizen of the United States nine years.

(*c*) Must be an inhabitant of the State from which he is elected.

9. After his election, a Senator may move from his State and still serve out his term.

10. If a Senator resigns, he directs his resignation to the Governor of his State.

11. Senators are elected by the State Legislatures as follows:

(*a*) On the *second Tuesday* after the meeting and organization of a Legislature preceding the expiration of the term of a Senator, each house votes separately for a Senator, each member, as his name is called, naming his candidate. The next day, at noon, both houses convene in joint session, and if the same person has received a majority of all the votes in each house, he is declared elected. If no person has received such majority, the joint assembly proceeds to choose a Senator by a *viva voce* vote. A majority of each house constitutes a quorum, and a majority of all votes cast elects.

(*b*) If no person is elected the first day, the joint assembly convenes daily at twelve o'clock, and takes at least one vote each day, during the session, or until a Senator is elected.

12. If a vacancy occurs when the Legislature is not in session, the Governor appoints a Senator to serve until the Legislature meets, when the unexpired term is filled regularly as above.

13. If a vacancy occurs while the Legislature is in session, the election occurs on the *second Tuesday* after the Legislature is notified of such vacancy.

14. Senators receive $5,000 each per year and 20 cents per mile going to and returning from Washington.

15. Each Senator is allowed a private Secretary at $100 per month.

16. The Vice-President administers the oath to Senators.

Privileged from arrest. (**48**); *Cannot hold other offices* (**866,2**).

726. Sessions of Congress.—*Regular Sessions*: The sessions of Congress beginning on the first Monday in December of each year. Each Congress holds two regular sessions.

2. *Long Session.*—The first regular session of Congress; so called because it may continue a whole year.

3. *Short Session.*—The second regular session of Congress—it must end by noon on the fourth day of March, when the new Congress comes into power. All work done on the fourth bears date of the third.

4. *Extra Session.*—A session of Congress held between the regular sessions.

(2) The President can convene one or both houses in extra session at pleasure.

(3) The Fortieth Congress held three extra sessions.

5. *Joint Session.*—A session of the two legislative branches organized as one body.

6. *Executive Session.*—A secret session of the

Senate held to confirm appointments made by the President, to ratify treaties, etc.

(2) On going into office, the President convenes the Senate in extra executive session to confirm his Cabinet.

727. Sheriff.—The chief executive officer of a county.

2. He has charge of the jail, serves writs, waits upon the court, and, in some States, collects taxes and acts as county treasurer.

728. Shire.—A county.

729. Siege.—The surrounding a place by an army for the purpose of compelling it to surrender.

730. Signal Service.—An organization connected with the War Department, that attends to the transmission of communications from a part of a battlefield or from one vessel in the Navy, by means of a system of signals.

2. Men are trained for the signal service at a special school at Fort Whipple, Virginia.

3. The Weather Bureau (**847**) is a division of this service.

731. Signal Station.—A station in the signal service (**730**) where observations are taken and signals are displayed.

732. Silver Bugs.—Those who favor the free coinage of silver (**364**).

733. Sine Die.—Without a day appointed; as to adjourn *sine die*—indefinitely.

734. Single Standard.—The use of gold alone or silver alone as a standard of money value.

735. Single Tax.—A proposed system of

raising *all* public revenues by a tax upon *land values alone*, irrespective of improvements.

736. Sinking Fund.—A fund set apart by the government, a State, or a corporation, to be applied to the reduction of its debt.

737. Sixteen-to-One.—An expression meaning that the mint value of sixteen ounces of silver shall be equal to the mint value of one ounce of gold; or that the pure silver in one silver dollar shall weigh as much as the pure gold in sixteen gold dollars.

738. Slander.—An oral, false, malicious statement about another, that injures him in his reputation or business.

2. It is not an indictable offense, but the person injured may recover damage in a civil suit (**785**).

3. He who knowingly repeats a slander, is liable the same as he who originates it.

4. If published, slander becomes libel (**478**).

739. Smithsonian Institution.—A scientific institution in Washington, organized by Congress, in 1846, agreeable to the provision of James Smithson, of England, who left $515,169 to the United States government "for the increase and diffusion of knowledge among men."

740. Smuggler.—(*a*) One who smuggles.

(*b*) A vessel employed in smuggling.

741. Smuggling.—Importing goods secretly to evade paying the legal duty thereon.

2. If detected, the smuggled goods are forfeited to the government, and the smuggler may be further punished.

742. Socialism.—A proposed system of industrial social reform which contemplates the social or collective, as opposed to the individual, ownership of the means of production; the collective management of production and the just and equitable distribution of products by society.

743. Solicitor General.—The chief assistant to the Attorney General (**324,4,2**).

744. Solvency.—Ability to pay all just debts as they fall due.

745. Sororicide.—(*a*) The crime of killing one's own sister.

(*b*) One who kills his own sister.

746. Sovereign.—The person, or body of persons, in whom the supreme executive and legislative power of a state is vested.

2 In limited monarchies, the king is usually called the sovereign, though he does not possess supreme power.

3. In the United States, the sovereign power is vested in the people, who act through their Representatives.

747. Sovereign State.—A state that administers its own government independently of any other state or government.

2. A sovereign state has (*a*) the absolute right to control its own members and (*b*) the absolute right to oppose interference in its affairs by any other state.

748. Sovereignty.—(*a*) Supreme power or dominion.

(*b*) A sovereign state.

749. Speaker.—The presiding officer of the

House of Representatives.

2. He is addressed as "Mr. Speaker."

3. His compensation is $8,000 and the usual mileage (**686,5**).

4. He is always a member of the House, and can therefore vote on all questions.

5. The Clerk of the previous House presides until the Speaker is elected.

6. Next to the President, he is the most powerful officer of the government, owing to his power to appoint the committees of the House, thus affecting legislation in a marked degree.

7. The above fact makes the election of Speaker exciting; in 1855-6, no Speaker was elected until the 2nd of February.

8. The title Speaker is also applied to the presiding officer of the lower house of a State Legislature, and to the presiding officer of the House of Commons.

750. Specie.—Money made of metal; coin.

751. Specie Payment.—The payment of obligations in coin.

752. Spoils System.—The practice of removing public officers and filling their places with active partisans from the ranks of the party in power.

2. The system originated in Pennsylvania and New York about the beginning of this century.

3. It was inaugurated as a national system by President Jackson, who removed about 2,000 the first year of his term, while the whole number removed up to that time, was

seventy-four.

4. The system is so called from "To the victors belong the spoils," spoken by W. L. Marcy, of New York, in the Senate in 1831.

753. Spy.—A secret agent who, in time of war, enters the enemy's camp ,or lines to ascertain and report his plans, strength, etc.

2. If caught in citizen's dress, or in the uniform of the camp in which he is found, he is, by international law, hanged without mercy. But if he wears the uniform of his own side, he is treated merely as a prisoner of war.

754. Squatter Sovereignty.—A phrase applied to the doctrine of pro-slavery men, that it should be left to the inhabitants of each territory to decide whether it should become a free State or a slave State.

755. Staff.—A body of officers attached to a superior officer, usually in the army, to assist him in carrying his plans into execution.

756. Stalwarts.—Those who stood boldly and firmly in the national convention of 1880, for Grant's election to the presidency a third time.

2. They were led by Rosco Conkling.

757. Stamp Act.—An Act of Parliament, 1765, taxing the Colonies through a stamp duty.

2. It was repealed in 1769, on account of the violent opposition of the colonists to "taxation without representation.

758. Stamp Act Congress.—A body of 27 delegates from nine of the Thirteen Colonies, which met in New York, Oct. 7-25, 1765.

2. It drew up a petition to the king, and

the Declaration of Rights or a "Declaration of Rights and Grievances of the Colonies of America," protesting against the Stamp Act and all attempts of Parliament to tax the colonists, and claiming for themselves all the rights of British subjects.

759. Standard Bullion.—Gold and silver bullion of the fineness of gold and silver coin dollars.

2. It contains 90 parts of pure gold or silver and 10 parts of copper alloy.

760. Star Chamber Sessions.— Any secret sessions. Sometimes applied to executive sessions of the Senate.

761. Star Route.—A postal line over which mail is carried in any other way than by railroad or steamboat; so called because such lines are indicated by stars on the books of the postal department.

762. Stars and Bars.—The flag of the Southern Confederacy during the Civil War.

763. Stars and Stripes.—A popular nickname for the United States flag (**350**).

764. State.—(*a*) A body politic (**94**); the whole body of people of a certain limited territory organized under the same government; a nation.

2. *State* and *government* are not synonymous terms; the state is all the people, while the government is a few persons intrusted with the ruling power. The government may be changed without changing the state. The government derives all its powers from the state.

(*b*) In the United States, one of the 45 commonwealths forming the Federal Union. *Powers of States*, (627). *Powers denied the States*. (870). *States' Rights*, (768).

765. State Courts.—The court systems of the different States vary so greatly that nothing better can be done than to give a general outline of the different courts.

2. The *Supreme Court* or *Court of Appeals* is the highest State Court, and consists of a Chief Justice and several Associate Judges.

(*2*) Every State has one Supreme Court.

(*3*) Its jurisdiction is generally appellate; but in some cases, it is original, and extends to both civil and criminal proceedings.

(*4*) It decides all State Constitutional questions.

(*5*) It decides questions of law; questions of fact coming up incidentally, are referred back to the lower courts for decision.

(*6*) All its decisions and opinions are published in bound volumes.

3. The *Circuit, Superior or District Court*, is inferior to the Supreme Court.

(*2*) Every State is divided into several circuits, each of which comprises several counties (sometimes one very large county may form a district) and in each circuit, a Judge is elected who is required to hold several stated sessions of court in each county of his circuit every year.

(*3*) Circuit Courts have original and appellate jurisdiction in both civil and criminal cases; they transact most of the judicial business of the State.

(*4*) Cases may be appealed from this court to the Supreme Court.

4. The *Probate, Surrogate,* or *Orphan's Court* is a court that attends to the proving of wills, and to the settlement of the estates of deceased persons.

(*2*) If a deceased person leaves no will, this court appoints an administrator (**11**).

(*3*) There is one court consisting of one Judge in each county.

(*4*) Appeals lie from this court to higher courts.

5. The *Justice's Court* is a court presided over by a Justice of the Peace (**454**).

(*2*) It is the oldest and humblest court in the land, and ofcourse it has original jurisdiction only.

(*3*) It tries petty criminal cases, and civil cases involving sums up to a certain amount varying in the different States.

6. The *Court of Impeachment* is the Senate sitting as a Court to try an impeachment (**404**) made against a public officer by the lower house.

7. The *Court of Oyer and Terminer* is a court that hears and determines criminal cases alone.

8. The *Court of Sessions* is, also, a court having criminal jurisdiction.

9. The *Police Court* is an inferior court held in a city or town for the trial of persons brought before it by the Police, charged with minor local offenses.

10. The *Court of Common Pleas* in most cases, is a county court having jurisdiction in civil cases only; in some States, however, it has both civil and criminal jurisdiction, which extends throughout the whole State.

11. The *Court of Equity or Court of Chancery* is a court for the trial of those peculiar cases for which the courts of law, owing to the deficiency of statutory law, provide no plain, adequate and complete remedy.

(*2*) This court does not change the written law; it simply supplies that wherein the law, on occount of its universality, is deficient, and applies it to the case in hand, as the circumstances and justice of the case may require.

(*3*) Only a few States have separate courts of chancery and of law; in most States, the same tribunal sits as a court of equity or as a law court, according to the nature of the case presented for adjudication.

766. State Government.—State government in the United States, resembles the national government; and he who understands well the latter, has a good general idea of the former, as the State may be considered as a miniature nation.

2. Each State has the three departments of government (**371**).

3. Each State has a Governor, a Supreme Court, and a Legislature consisting of two branches.

4. In eleven States, the legislative body is called the General Assembly.

5. In Massachusetts and New Hampshire,

it is called the General Court.

6. States differ somewhat in the names and number of officers, terms of office, and salaries

7. It would require to much space to describe each State government separately.

8. A knowledge of the government of one's own State will give the student an idea sufficiently full and accurately.

767. Statesman.—A man engaged in public affairs, who is well versed in the science and art of government, and who possesses marked political abilities.

768. States' Rights.—The rights of the individual States as such, as distinguished from the rights of the Federal government.

2. The phrase is usually applied to the doctrine that States could individually nullify acts of Congress, or secede from the Union at pleasure.

769. Statute.—A positive law enacted by a legislative body. An enactment.

770. Statute Law.—The written law. The acts passed by representative legislative assemblies.

2. In all cases where Statute and Common Law conflict, the Statute Law takes precedence.

771. Statute of Frauds.—An old English statute (1676) requiring certain contracts and agreements to be in writing in order to be legally binding; for example, a contract that can not be performed within a year must be reduced to writing to be legally binding.

14

2. The statute of frauds in various forms, is in force in all the States except Pennsylvania.

772. Statute of Limitations.—A statute preprescribing the time within which an action at law must be commenced in order to enforce rights.

773. Strike.—The agreement of a body of workmen to do no more work until their employer complies with certain demands made by them.

774. Struck Jury.—A special jury composed of men who, on account of their occupation, etc., are especially qualified to decide a special case.

2. For such a jury, 48 names are selected. From this list the contending parties alternately strike off 12 names, and the remaining 24 are summoned, and from this number the jury is regularly impanelled.

775. Stuffing the Ballot Box.—Putting fraudulent votes into the ballot box for the purpose of giving one party an unfair advantage.

776. Stump Speech.—A political harangue made in a campaign for the purpose of winning votes.

2. It is so called from the fact that in early colonial times, the political orator used a stump for his platform.

777. Subaltern.—A commissioned military officer inferior in rank to a captain; that is, a Lieutenant.

778. Subject.—A citizen; one owing allegiance to a sovereign or to a sovereign state.

779. Subornation.—The act of bribing or persuading a person (a) to commit perjury, or (b) to do any criminal act.

780. Subpoena.—(a) A writ or process ordering a witness, under penalty, to appear in a court of justice and testify.

(b) A process or writ commanding a defendant in equity to appear and answer the plaintiff's bill.

781. Subsidiary Coin.—Silver coin of less value than one dollar.

2. They are legal tender for any sum not exceeding ten dollars.

782. Subsidy.—(a) Money or other aid granted by the Nation, a State, or a municipal government, to a private individual or a corporation, to aid in establishing or maintaining a private enterprise that will be of special benefit to the public; as to grant a subsidy to a railroad, etc.

(b) Money paid by one government to another for the purpose of securing the aid or neutrality of the latter in time of war.

2. A subsidy differs from a tribute in that the former is voluntary, while the latter is demanded or exacted.

783. Suffrage.—Vote; expression of choice.

784. Suffragist.—A voter.

785. Suit, Cause, Action or Case.—An action prosecuted in a court of justice by one party against another, to recover, enforce or protect a right, or to punish or prevent a wrong.

2. A *civil suit* is a suit between persons, real or fictitious (*corporations*), to recover, enforce or protect a right, where no crime is

alleged.

3. A *criminal suit*, in which a State or the United States is always the plaintiff, is an action brought against a person for committing a crime (**247**) or a misdemeanor (**523**).

4. A *suit in equity* is a suit brought in a chancery court (**765,**11) to enforce a right not definitely provided for by statutory law.

786. Summons.—A legal notice to a defendant to appear in court at a specified time to answer to the demands of a plaintiff.

787. Supreme Court, U. S.—The highest court of the land, from whose decision there is no appeal.

2. It consists of one Chief Justice and eight Associate Justices (**340**).

3. It holds one annual session each year in the capitol at Washington, convening on the second Monday in October.

4. Six of the Judges constitute a quorum, and the agreement of a majority stands as the decision of the court.

5. Each of the nine Justices is appointed to one of the Federal Circuits (**146,**4), where, by law, he is required to hold one session in two years.

6. It has original jurisdiction only in cases affecting ambassadors, other public ministers and consuls, and in cases in which a State is a party. In all other cases, it has only appellate jurisdiction—that is, it reviews cases appealed from the inferior courts.

7. Its appellate jurisdiction is subject to exemptions and regulations made by Congress.

which may and does, provide for the final disposition of certain classes of cases in inferior courts.

8. It appoints its own Marshal, or Federal sheriff; a Clerk, and a Reporter who edits and publishes its decisions.

9. It has no juries.

10. It can modify or reverse its own decisions.

11. Any case whatever involving the interpretation of the Constitution can be appealed to the Supreme Court.

12. Cases may be, appealed to this court from the Supreme Courts of the Territories and of the District of Columbia.

13. A case can not be appealed from a State court to the Supreme Court, except on the ground that the decision of the State court conflicts with the Constitution or with the Federal laws.

788. Supreme Law of the Land.—The Constitution, the Statutes of Congress, and all treaties made under the authority of the United States.

789. Surrogate.—A Probate Judge (765,4).

790. Tariff.—(*a*) A schedule or table of duties charged on the imports or exports of a country.

(*b*) The duty, or the rate of duty, charged on imports or exports.

2. The United States and Great Britain impose duties only on imports.

3. Tariff on exports is forbidden by the Constitution.

4. Tariff must be paid in gold by the im-

porter.

5. *Protective tariff* is tariff laid on imported goods for the purpose of protecting and encouraging home industries.

(*1*) The first protective tariff act was passed July, 1789.

(*2*) Canada, Australia, and most continental countries have protective tariffs.

6. *Revenue tariff* is tariff laid on certain goods solely to raise money for the support of the government.

7. Congress alone can impose a tariff on goods.   *Exception*, (870, 2).

8. Under the Confederation, the States passed tariff laws.

791. Tariff of Abominations.—The very high protective tariff of 1828.

792. Tax.—Money levied and collected by the government for public purposes.

2. A *direct tax* is paid directly by the taxpayer to the government.

3. An *indirect tax* is paid directly by the owner of goods, and then later by the purchaser.

4. TAXES.— { *Direct* { Poll Tax. / Property Tax. } *Indirect* { Duties or Customs. / Excises or Int. Rev. } }

5. The national government usually raises all its revenue by indirect taxes.

6. State and local governments raise revenue mainly by direct taxation.

7. When the national government levies a direct tax, it must be apportioned among the

States and Territories according to population. This was done in 1798, 1813, 1815, 1816, and 1861.

8. No poll tax has ever been levied by the general government.

9. Under the Articles of Confederation (52), Congress could not collect taxes; it could only ask the States to do so.

10. Certain kinds of property are usually exempt from taxation—all public property, cemeteries, charitable, humane and educational institutions, churches, etc.

11. The only limit to the taxing power of Congress is that it cannot levy a tax on exports.

Income Tax, (411); *Single Tax*, (735).

793. Teller.—A person appointed to count the votes cast in a legislative or other assembly.

794. Tenure.—The act, right or manner of holding real estate.

795. Tenure of Office Bill.—A bill providing that persons holding, or appointed to any civil office by and with the consent of the Senate, should be entitled to hold such office until a successor should be. in like manner, appointed and duly qualified.

2. It was passed in 1867, over President Johnson's veto, and was repealed in 1887.

3. In 1868, President Johnson was impeached mainly for violating this act.

4. The President can now remove his appointees at will.

796. Territorial Sea.—The waters of the

ocean off the coast of any country to the distance of three miles, is the territorial sea of
that particular country.

797. Territory.—A definite portion of a
country, organized with a government under
the direction and control of Congress, and not
yet having been admitted into the Union as a
State.

2. When a territory is organized, the President, with the consent of the Senate, appoints
a Governor, a Secretary, a Chief Justice and
two Associate Justices of the Supreme Court,
an Attorney and a Marshal, for the term of four
years, unless sooner removed by the President.

3. All other territorial officers are appointed by the Governor with the advice and consent of the Council or territorial Senate.

4. Justices of the Peace and military officers
are elected; all other township, district and
county officers are either appointed or elected
as provided for by the Governor and the Legislature.

5. Every Territory is divided into three judicial districts, in which the three Supreme Judges singly hold District Courts.

6. The Supreme Court must hold one term
annually at the seat of government of the Territory.

7. The Supreme Court has appellate jurisdiction over cases decided by the District
Courts.

8. Inferior Courts are established by the territorial Legislature, which is elected.

9. The salaries of territorial officers are as

follows:

(*1*) Governor, $3,500 per year.

(*2*) Secretary, $2,500 per year.

(*3*) Supreme Judges, $3,000 per year.

(*4*) Attorney, $250 per year and fees.

(*5*) Marshal, $200 per year and fees.

(*6*) President of the Council and Speaker of the House of Representatives, $10 per day and mileage.

(*7*) Other Legislators, $6 per day and mileage.

10. Territorial officers are paid quarterly out of the United States Treasury.

11. The Legislature makes the laws, but they must be submitted to Congress for approval before they become effective, as Congress has supreme control over territorial governments.

12. Territories have no Senators nor Representatives in Congress, but each Territory elects one Delegate to the House of Representatives. He may debate and serve on committees, but he can not vote.

13. A Delegate receives $5,000 per year and the usual mileage.

14. All the States except Maine, Vermont, West Virginia, California, Texas and the Thirteen Original States, had territorial governments at one time.

15 There are three organized Territories governed as above, viz., Arizona, New Mexico and Oklahoma.

16. EXCEPTIONS.—*Alaska* has a Governor and a District Court, but no Legislature.

(*2*) Congress provides that the laws of Oregon, when not conflicting with those of the United States. shall be the laws of Alaska.

17. *Indian Territory* is governed by the Indians.

(*2*) It has no Legislature.

(*3*) Each tribe makes and executes its own laws.

(*4*) Crimes committed against white persons are punished in the United States courts in adjoining States.

18. The *District of Columbia* is governed directly by Congress.

(*2*) Three Commissioners appointed by the President and confirmed by the Senate. administer its affairs.

(*3*) Unlike the Territories, it can never become a State.

(*4*) It has no Delegates in Congress, and its citizens do not vote.

(5) The Supreme Court of the District of Columbia, consists of one Chief Justice at a salary of $4,500 per year, and five Associate Justices at a salary of $4,000 each per year, all of whom are appointed by the President with the consent of the Senate.

(6) These Judges hold office during good behavior.

(7) The Court has general appellate and original jurisdiction within the District, and an appeal lies to the United States Supreme Court.

19. A territorial government is temporary; the object being to prepare the Territory for

admission into the Union as a State.

798. Territorial Growth of the United States. —*Original.*—1783. The Thirteen Original States and the Northwest Territory. By treaty with Great Britain. Boundaries: *East*, Atlantic Ocean: *South*, the northern line of Florida to the Mississippi River; *West*, the Mississippi River; *North*, the Great Lakes.

(2) Total area, 830,000 square miles.

2. *Louisiana Purchase.*—1803. By purchase from France for $15,000,000; over 1,000,000 square miles.

(2) It extended from the Gulf of Mexico to Canada, and from the Mississippi River to the Rocky Mountains ˙ on the west, being the width of the present State of Louisiana on the South.

3. *Florida.*—1819. By purchase from Spain, for $15,000,000.

4. *Texas.*—1845. By annexation, upon condition that it should be divided into five separate States whenever the people of the State desired it to be done.

5. *Oregon Country.*—1846. By discovery, exploration and treaty.

(2) Boundaries: *North*, Canada; *East*, the Rocky Mountains; *South*, the northern line of California to the Rocky Mountains; *West*, the Pacific Ocean.

6. *First Mexican Cession.*—1848. By conquest from Mexico, the United States paying Mexico $15,000,000, and assuming $3,000,000 that Mexico owed citizens of the United States.

(*2*) It extended from the "Oregon Country" to the Gila River, and from the Rocky Mountains to the Pacific Ocean.

7. *Gadsden Purchase*, or *Second Mexican Cession.*—1853. By purchase from Mexico for $10,000,000.

(*2*) The territory lying between the Gila River and the present boundary between the United States and Mexico.

8. *Alaska.*—1867. By purchase from Russia for $7,200,000.

9. *Hawaii.*—1898. By annexation.

10. *Porto Rico, the Philippine and other Islands.*—1898. By conquest from Spain.

799. Testate.—One who leaves a legally executed will at death.

800. Testator.—A man who leaves a will at death.

801. Testatrix.—A woman who leaves a will at death.

802. Teste.—(*a*) A witness.

(*b*) The witnessing clause at the close of any document.

803. Third Parties.—Applied to all other parties except the two leading (Democratic and Republican) parties.

804. Theft.—Larceny (463).

805. Theftbote.—The receiving by the owner, goods stolen from him, or compensation for the same, on his agreement not to prosecute the thief.

806. Three-Fifths Rule.—A compromise effected in the Constitutional Convention of 1787 (**217,2,3**) whereby Representatives in Congress and direct taxes were apportioned among the several States according to population, which was to be determined by adding to the whole number of free persons, (excepting Indians not taxed) three-fifths of all other persons (slaves); that is, all of the white and three-fifths of the slaves were to be counted, or, five slaves were to be counted as three persons (**862,**3).

2. Slavery having been abolished, this rule is now void.

3. Under the Articles of Confederation, each State had one vote in Congress, and was taxed according to its value in real estate.

807. Tie Vote.—An equal number of votes cast for each candidate, or for and against a given proposition.

808. Title.—An appellation of honor, distinction or dignity conferred upon, or inherited by, persons.

2. Neither Congress nor the States can confer titles of honor and distinction.

3. In Great Britain, the grade of titles is as follows, beginning with the highest: Prince, Duke, Marquis, Earle, Viscount, Baron, Baronet, and Knight.

809. Token Money.—Any money that legally passes for more than its real value; as a cent piece, the metal in which is not worth its face value; or paper money.

810. Tonnage.—(a) The carrying capacity of a vessel in tons.

(b) A duty or tax on vessels in proportion

to their carrying capacity in tons.

2. Congress alone can levy tonnage duties.

3. The first Congress levied tonnage duties, which were modified from time to time, until now we have no such duties.

§11. Tonnage Duties.—Taxes levied on ships according to the number of tons freight they can carry.

3. States can not levy tonnage duties without the consent of Congress. Such consent has never been given to the States.

§12. Trade Dollar.—A Silver dollar containing 420 grains, coined in 1873, for commercial use in Asia.

2. Though containing more silver than a standard silver dollar, it continued to be a legal tender here only until 1876.

3. In 1887, Congess authorized standard silver dollars to be given in exchange for them.

813. Trade Mark.—A trade mark is a special device or mark adopted by a manufacturer or dealer to distinguish his goods.

2. Trade marks are registered in the Patent Office, from which, circulars of information can be obtained, on request, at any time.

3. A trade mark is granted for 30 years, and is renewable for another 30 years, on application within six months prior to the expiration of the original term.

4. In order to secure protection, the words *"Trade Mark"* must be placed in close proximity to the original device.

5. The fee for a trade mark or a renewal is $25.

6. Prior to 1879, trade marks were patented; but the Supreme Court then decided that they were not patentable.

814. Traitor.—One who betrays his country: one who commits treason. One who by any means seeks the downfall of his country.

2. Traitors are punished by death.

815. Treason.—(*a*) Levying war against the United States, or (*b*) adhering to their enemies, giving aid and comfort to them.

2. No person shall be convicted of treason unless on the testimony of two witnesses to the same overt act, or on confession in open court.

3. To constitute treason, war must be actually levied. Simply a conspiracy to overthrow the government, is not treason.

4. Congress names the punishment, which is death, or imprisonment for not less than five years and a fine of not less than $10,000, at the discretion of the court.

5. No attainder of treason shall work corruption of blood (**233**), or forfeiture, except during the life of the person attained; that is, no innocent relative shall suffer in any way for the treasonable act of another.

6. There can be no treason against a particular State, because it is not a sovereign power.

7. The United States Supreme Court tries cases of treason.

816. Treasury Notes.—Notes issued and circulated by the government, which are mere promises of the government to pay—mere ev-

idences of debt due by the government to the
holders of the notes.

2. Some are legal tender and some are not.
Greenbacks are legal tender treasury notes.

817. Treaty.—A compact or agreement between two or more nations, in regard to commerce, peace, boundaries, mutual protection,
or any other matter.

2. The President alone, with the concurrence
of the Senate (872,2), has power to make
treaties.

3. In negotiating the terms of a treaty, the
President acts through the Secretary of State,
a foreign minister, or commissioners appointed for the special purpose.

4. When the terms are agreed upon, the
treaty is signed by the representatives of the
nations concerned, and then submitted to
their respective governments for ratification.

5. Until ratified as above, no treaty is binding.

6. It requires a two-thirds vote of the Senate (the members present) to ratify a treaty.

7. When properly ratified by all the governments interested, the President, by proclamation, makes the treaty public.

8. The Constitution prohibits States from
making treaties.

818. Trial.—The formal judicial examination into a case in a regular court of justice
to determine the questions or charges in issue.

2. Criminal trials are held in the States
where the crimes are committed.

3. A crime committed on the high seas is

tried in the State where the vessel on which it is committed first lands.

4. Civil cases are tried in the proper courts of the States where they originate (**765**).

819. Tribute.—A valuable consideration, or an annual or stated sum of money paid by one country or ruler to another as an acknowledgment of submission, or to purchase peace or protection.

820. Truce.—A temporary suspension of hostilities, by agreement, for negotiating terms of peace, etc.

2. A flag of truce is a white flag displayed by one of the contending parties, during the flying of which, all hostilities cease.

821. Trustee.—One intrusted with property for the use of another.

822. Tweed Ring.—1860-1871. A p o l i t i c a l ring composed of Wm. M. Tweed, A. O. Hall, P. B. Sweeney, and R. B. Connolly.

2. The ring ruled New York City by corruption, fraud and bribery, stealing millions of dollars, and increasing the city debt $81,000,000.

3. The ring was broken up by the efforts of Samuel J. Tilden.

4. Tweed died in prison under a sentence of twelve years. The other three members left the country.

823. Ultimatum.—The final decision of a government on a given subject; the best terms or the final proposition it will offer another government in a diplomatic negotiation.

15

824. Uncle Sam.—A nickname for the United States government.

2. The name originated thus: Samuel Wilson, an inspector of provisions at Troy, New York, in the War of 1812, was familiarly known among his friends as "Uncle Sam." One day, goods were received for a government contractor named Elbert Anderson, which were marked "E. A., U. S." One of the men mistook these initials to mean "Elbert Anderson and Uncle Sam."

825. Unconstitutional Laws.—Laws that conflict with the requirements of a constitution.

2. A national law or a State law is always valid until declared unconstitutional by the United States Supreme Court or the State Supreme Court, respectively.

3. The United States Supreme Court has pronounced but four laws unconstitutional, as follows:

(*a*) In 1801, an *Act of 1789* that gave the Supreme Court original jurisdiction not warranted by the Constitution.

(*b*) In 1857, section eight of the *Missouri Compromise*, prohibiting slavery north of 36° 30′—The Dred Scott Decision.

(*c*) In 1867, that part of the *Test Oath* of 1862 and 1865 that applied to attorneys practicing in United States Courts prior to the Civil War—a bill of attainder and *ex post facto* law.

(*d*) In 1894, the *Income Tax of 1894*, on the ground that it was a direct tax and could be levied by Congress only by apportioning it among the States according to population. The judges stood five to four.

4. The court in no case passes upon the constitutionality of a law unless it be required to do so in a case.

826. Union.—The 45 United States of America inseparably banded together in one government.

2. Territories belong to, but are not in, the Union.

827. Union Party.—The party that opposed Secession in the Civil War.

828. Unit Rule.—A rule requiring a body to vote as a unit; as States formerly voted in National Conventions, and in Congress under the Articles of Confederation.

829. Universal Postal Union.—A union of most of the civilized countries of the world, providing for a uniform rate of postage on mail matter carried from one country of the Union to another.

2. Within the Union, the postage on letters is 5 cents per half ounce, and postal cards are two cents each. Other mail matter is carried at uniform rates.

3. The Union was organized in 1874; its central office is located in Switzerland, and is under the control of that government.

4. The expenses of the Union are paid by contributions from the nations belonging to it.

5. The United States belongs to the Union.

830. Unlawful Oath.—An oath binding one to do some unlawful thing; as to commit murder, treason, etc.; generally taken by members of illegal societies, as the "Ku-Klux Klan."

831. Usury.—A higher rate of interest on money than is allowed by law.

832. Venire.—A judicial writ directing a sheriff to cause a certain number of qualified citizens to appear in court at a certain time to serve on the jury.

833. Venue.—The county or place where a crime is committed and in which the offense must, legally, be tried.

2. A *change of venue* is an order of a court directing the trial of a criminal to be held in a different county from that in which the crime was committed.

3. A change of venue is allowed when a criminal is not likely to get a fair trial in his own county.

834. Verdict.—The unanimous decision of a jury in a civil or criminal cause legally tried before them.

2. A court may on various grounds set aside a verdict and grant a new trial, except in the case of one regularly acquitted of a charge of crime. Such a person cannot be placed in jeopardy a second time (**437**).

835. Veto (*I forbid*).—The power of a chief executive to prevent the enactment of measures passed by a legislative body.

2. If the President vetoes a bill, he must return it to the house in which it originated, with his written objections, which are entered on the journal of that house.

3. To become a law, a vetoed bill must pass both houses by a two-thirds yea and nay vote (859) of all the members of each house.

4. In all the States except Ohio, Deleware, North-Carolina and Rhode Island, the Governor possesses the veto power.

5. In thirteen States, the Governor can veto some items in an appropriation bill, and approve others.

6. In the States, from a mere majority vote, as in West Virginia, to a three-fifths vote, is required to pass a bill over the Governor's veto.

7. In England, the executive has a veto power, but now never exercises it.

8. In the States, a vetoed bill is returned to the house that originates it, except in Kansas, where it must always be returned to the lower house.

836. Vice-President.—The person elected to fill the office of President in case a vacancy occurs in that office, or in case the Electors fail to elect a President and ther the House of Representatives fail to elect one before the fourth of March.

2. His term of office is four years.

3. His salary is $8,000 per year.

4. He is *ex officio* (**329**) President of the Senate, but has no vote except in case of tie.

5. He cannot preside over the Senate when the President is impeached (**404,6**).

6. He is elected by the Electors like the President (**302,9**).

7. The qualifications for Vice-President are the same as for President (**636,7**).

8. There is no provision for filling a vacancy in the office of Vice-President.

9. If the Electors fail to elect a Vice-President, then the Senate proceeds at once to elect one from the two candidates having the two highest numbers of votes (896,2).

10. Two-thirds of the whole number of Senators constitute a quorum to elect a Vice-President, and a majority of the whole number is necessary to a choice.

11. In the election of 1836, Richard M. Johnson was elected Vice-President by the Senate, to serve with Martin Van Buren. Johnson was the only Vice-President elected by the Senate.

12. Originally, there were no candidates for Vice-President; but all were cndidates for President, and the two that received the highest and next highest numbers of votes, were President and Vice-President respectively.

13. The Vice-President is inaugurated immediately before the President.

837. Viva Voce Vote.—Any oral vote; a vote in which all favoring a measure answer together, *Aye* or *Yes*, and all opposing it answer *Nay* or *No*, the presiding officer deciding the vote by his ear.

838. Volunteer.—One who voluntarily becomes a member of the organized militia (514,3), as distinguished from a regular (682) or a soldier of the standing army (44,2).

839. Vote.—Expression of choice or preference.

Majority Vote, (**491**); *Minority Vote*, (**521**); *Casting Vote*, (**132**); *Yea and Nay Vote*,(**859**); *Vote by Acclamation*, (**4**); *Cumulative Vote*, (**251**).

840. Voter.—An elector (**301**); a suffragist; one who has a legal right to vote.

2. The qualifications for voting are left entirely to the individual States. They can restrict suffrage in any way they please.

Proviso, (**898,2**).

841. Wager.—A bet. The staking of money or property between two parties on the chance of something happening or not happening.

2. Money on bets cannot be recovered by law.

842. War.—An armed conflict between nations.

2. The power to declare war is vested in Congress.

3. A State cannot engage in war without the consent of Congress unless (*a*) actually invaded, or (*b*) in such imminent danger as will not admit of delay.

4. Congress did not declare war in 1861, but passed "An act to authorize the employment of volunteers to aid in enforcing the laws and protecting public property."

5. An *offensive war* is one first begun by a nation against another nation.

6. A *defensive war* is one instituted by a nation in its defense against another nation that has already begun war against it.

843. Ward.—One of the smaller divisions in

to which a city or town is divided for convenience of local government.

844. War Governors.—The State Governors during the Civil War, who so promptly responded to President Lincoln's call for soldiers.

845. Warrant.—A document issued by a magistrate or justice, commanding an officer to make an arrest, to seize certain property, or to search certain premises.

2. It is issued upon the sworn complaint of some interested person, and sets forth the nature of the crime complained of.

846. Warranty.—The express or implied agreement of a person to be held responsible if a certain fact relating to the subject of a contract is not, or shall not be, exactly as represented by him.

847. Weather Bureau or Meteorological Bureau.—A division of the signal service (730) that forecasts probable changes of the weather for twenty-four hours in advance and notifies the people through the newspapers, post offices and signal stations.

2. Observations are taken three times a day at nearly five hundred signal stations distributed throughout the country, and telegraphed as nearly the same time as possible to the central office at Washington, where the forecasts are made.

3. About 83 per cent. of the predictions made twenty-four hours in advance, are correct.

4. This bureau was transferred in 1891, to the Department of Agriculture.

848. Weights and Measures.—Congress has power to fix the standard of weights and measures, but has never done so.

2. But it has adopted the English standard for use in the customhouses, and has furnished exact copies of these to the States, all of which have adopted them.

849. White House or Executive Mansion.— The house in which the President lives during his term of office.

2. It is the first public building erected in Washington.

3. It is built of white marble; hence its name.

4. It is situated about a mile from the National Capitol.

5. Here the President has his office and transacts all his official duties.

850. White League or Invisible Empire.—The Ku-Klux Klan (**461**).

851. Wild Cat Money.—Unsound money issued by banks and not redeemed.

852. Will or Testament.—A written instrument in which the writer declares his will concerning the disposal of his property after his death.

2. A will must be signed by two or more witnesses, in whose presence the testator (**800**) must sign or acknowledge it.

3. In some States, as in West Virginia, a holographic will (**391**) does not require witnesses.

4. A will may be revoked—

   (*1*) By destroying it,

   (*2*) By disposing of the property willed, or

(*3*) By executing another will in which the former is expressly revoked.

5. There is no set form of words in which a will must be written.

6. To be valid, a will must be made by one of sound mind and disposing memory.

7. A will must always be written, except in a few States, where personal property to certain amounts may be willed orally, and except in the case of soldiers and sailors in active service, who may always dispose of personal property, but not of real estate, orally or by nuncupative will (**561**).

8. A person *devises* real estate, and *bequeaths* personal property.

853. Wire Pulling.—Artful activity exercised by politicians to secure votes for a candidate or for a measure.

854. Without Recourse.—A phrase added to the indorsement on a note, etc., releasing the indorser from all liability to subsequent holders.

855. Witness.—(*a*) One who gives evidence in a case before a court.

(*b*) One who signs any written instrument for the purpose of confirming its authenticity.

2. A *privileged* witness is one who is not compelled to testify in regard to certain official and professional matters; as State officers, lawyers, physicians and ministers, who are not obliged to divulge official and professional secrets.

856. Woman Suffrage.—The right of women to vote.

2. Women can vote on various local questions in 24 States.

3. In Wyoming, Colorado and Utah, women have equal suffrage with men. They can hold office and vote for all officers from Presidential Electors down.

857. Writ.—A written instrument under seal, issued by a court, commanding the performance or the nonperformance of a specified act by the person to whom it is directed.

858. Writs of Assistance.—Search warrants authorizing English officers to enter stores and private dwellings to search for foreign merchandise on which duty had not been paid, and to compel the sheriff to aid them in their work.

859. Yea and Nay Vote.—A vote taken by calling the roll, each member voting as his name is called, the object being to make an official record of how each member votes.

2. One-fifth of the members present can demand the yeas and nays in Congress (**865,3**).

THE

CONSTITUTION

OF THE

UNITED STATES OF AMERICA

[*Ratified by the States 1787-1790.*]

Preamble.

[860] We, the people of the United States, in order to (1) form a more perfect union, (2) establish justice, (3) insure domestic tranquillity, (4) provide for the common defense, (5) promote the general welfare, and (6) secure the blessings of liberty to ourselves and our posterity, do ordain and establish this Constitution for the United States of America.

ARTICLE I.—Legislative Department.

· [861] SECTION 1.—*Congress in General.*

All legislative powers herein granted shall be vested in a Congress of the United States, which shall consist of a Senate and a House of Representatives.

[862] SECTION 2.—*House of Representatives.*

1. Election.—The House of Representatives shall be composed of members chosen every second year by the people of the several States; and the electors in each State shall have the qualifications requisite for electors

of the most numerous branch of the State
Legislature.

2. *Qualifications.*—No person shall be a Representative who shall not (1) have attained
to the age of twenty-five years, and (2) been
seven years a citizen of the United States, and
who shall not (3) when elected, be an inhabitant of that State in which he shall be chosen.

3. *Apportionment.*—Representatives and direct taxes shall be apportioned among the
several States which may be included within
this Union, according to their respective
numbers, which shall be determined by adding
to the whole number of free persons, including
those bound to service for a term of years,
and excluding Indians not taxed, three-fifths
of all other persons. The actual enumeration
shall be made within three years after the
first meeting of the Congress of the United
States, and within every subsequent term of
ten years, in such manner as they shall by law
direct. The number of Representatives shall
not exceed one for every thirty thousand, but
each State shall have at least one Representative; and until such enumeration shall be
made, the State of New Hampshire shall be
entitled to choose three, Massachusetts eight,
Rhode Island and Providence Plantations one,
Connecticut five, New York six, New Jersey
four, Pennsylvania eight, Delaware one,
Maryland six, Virginia ten, North Carolina
five, South Carolina five, and Georgia three.

4. *Vacancies.*—When vacancies happen in
the representation from any State, the execu-

tive authority thereof shall issue writs of election to fill such vacancies.

5. Officers.—The House of Representatives shall choose their Speaker and other officers, and shall have the sole power of impeachment.

[863]   SECTION 3.—*Senate.*

1. Election.—The Senate of the United States shall be composed of two Senators from each State, chosen by the Legislature thereof for six years, and each Senator shall have one vote.

2. Classes, etc.—Immediately after they shall be assembled in consequence of the first election, they shall be divided, as equally as may be, into three classes. The seats of the Senators of the first class shall be vacated at the expiration of the second year; of the second class, at the expiration of the fourth year; and of the third class, at the expiration of the sixth year, so that one-third may be chosen every second year; and if vacancies happen by resignation or otherwise during the recess of the Legislature of any State, the executive thereof may make temporary appointments until the next meeting of the Legislature, which shall then fill such vacancies.

3. *Qualifications.*—No person shall be a Senator who shall not have (1) attained the age of thirty years, and (2) been nine years a citizen of the United States, and who shall not (3), when elected, be an inhabitant of that State from which he shall be chosen.

4. Presiding Officer.—The Vice-President of

the United States shall be President of the Senate, but shall have no vote, unless they be equally divided.

5. President pro tempore.—The Senate shall choose their other officers, and also a President *pro tempore* in the absence of the Vice-President, or when he shall exercise the office of President of the United States.

6. Impeachments.—The Senate shall have the sole power to try all impeachments. When sitting for that purpose, they shall be on oath or affirmation. When the President of the United States is tried, the Chief Justice shall preside; and no person shall be convicted without the concurrence of two-thirds of the members present.

7. Judgment.—Judgment in cases of impeachment shall not extend further than to removal from office, and disqualification to hold and enjoy any office of honor, trust or profit under the United States; but the party convicted shall, nevertheless, be liable and subject to indictment, trial, judgment, and punishment, according to law.

[**864**]   SECTION 4.—*Both Houses.*

1. Election.—The times, places, and manner of holding elections for Senators and Representatives shall be prescribed in each State by the Legislature thereof; but the Congress may at any time, by law, make or alter such regulations, except as to the place of choosing Senators.

2. Meetings.—The Congress shall assemble at least once in every year, and such meeting shall be on the first Monday in December, unless they shall by law appoint a different day.

[865] SECTION 5.—*Houses Separately.*

1. Quorum.—Each house shall be the judge of the elections, returns, and qualifications of its own members, and a majority of each shall constitute a quorum to do business; but a smaller number may adjourn from day to day, and may be authorized to compel the attendance of absent members, in such manner and under such penalties as each house may provide.

2. Rules.—Each house may determine the rules of its proceedings, punish its members for disorderly behavior, and, with the concurrence of two-thirds, expel a member.

3. Journal.—Each house shall keep a journal of its proceedings, and from time to time publish the same, excepting such parts as may in their judgment require secrecy; and the yeas and nays of the members of either house, on any question, shall, at the desire of one-fifth of those present, be entered on the journal.

4. Adjournment.—Neither house during the session of Congress shall, without the consent of the other, adjourn for more than three days, nor to any other place than that in which the two houses shall be sitting.

[866] SECTION 6.—*Members as Individuals.*

1. Pay and Privileges.—The Senators and Representatives shall receive a compensation for their services, to be ascertained by law, and paid out of the treasury of the United States. They shall in all cases except treason, felony, and breach of the peace, be privileged from arrest during their attendance at the session of their respective houses, and in going to and returning from the same; and for any speech or debate in either house they shall not be questioned in any other place.

2. *Prohibitions.*—No Senator or Representative shall, during the time for which he was elected, be appointed to any civil office under the authority of the United States, which shall have been created, or the emoluments whereof shall have been increased, during such time; and no person holding any office under the United States shall be a member of either house during his continuance in office.

[867] SECTION 7.—*Revenue; The Veto.*

1. *Revenue Bills.*—All bills for raising revenue shall originate in the House of Representatives; but the Senate may propose or concur with amendments as on other bills.

2. *The Veto.*—Every bill which shall have passed the House of Representatives and the Senate, shall, before it becomes a law, be presented to the President of the United States; if he approve, he shall sign it; but if not, he shall return it, with his objections, to that house in which it shall have originated; who shall enter the objections at large on their journal, and proceed to reconsider it. If, after such reconsideration, two-thirds of that house shall agree to pass the bill, it shall be

16

sent, together with the objections, to the other house, by which it shall likewise be reconsidered; and, if approved by two-thirds of that house, it shall become a law. But in all cases, the votes of both houses shall be determined by yeas and nays, and the names of the persons voting for and against the bill shall be entered on the journal of each house respectively. If any bill shall not be returned by the President within ten days (Sundays excepted) after it shall have been presented to him, the same shall be a law in like manner as if he had signed it, unless the Congress, by their adjournment, prevent its return, in which case it shall not be a law.

3. Every order, resolution or vote, to which the concurrence of the Senate and the House of Representatives may be necessary (except on a question of adjournment), shall be presented to the President of the United States; and, before the same shall take effect, shall be approved by him; or, being disapproved by him, shall be repassed by two-thirds of the Senate and House of Representatives, according to the rules and limitations prescribed in the case of a bill.

[868] SECTION 8.—*Legislative Powers.*

The Congress shall have power:

1. To lay and collect taxes, duties, imposts, and excises; to pay the debts and provide for the common defense and general welfare of the United States; but all duties, imposts and excises shall be uniform throughout the United States.

2. To borrow money on the credit of the United States.

3. To regulate commerce with foreign nations, and among the several States, and with the Indian tribes.

4. To establish a uniform rule of naturalization, and uniform laws on the subject of bankruptcies throughout the United States.

5. To coin money, regulate the value thereof, and of foreign coin, and fix the standard of weights and measures.

6. To provide for the punishment of counterfeiting the securities and current coin of the United States.

7. To establish postoffices and postroads.

8. To promote the progress of science and useful arts, by securing for limited times, to authors and inventors the exclusive right to their respective writings and discoveries.

9. To constitute tribunals inferior to the Supreme Court.

10. To define and punish piracies and felonies committed on the high seas, and offenses against the law of nations.

11. To declare war, grant letters of marque and reprisal, and make rules concerning captures on land and water.

12. To raise and support armies; but no appropriation of money to that use shall be for a longer term than two years.

13. To provide and maintain a navy.

14. To make rules for the government and regulation of the land and naval forces.

15. To provide for calling forth the militia

to execute the laws of the Union, suppress insurrections, and repel invasions.

16. To provide for organizing, arming and disciplining the militia, and for governing such part of them as may be employed in the service of the United States; reserving to the States respectively the appointment of the officers and the authority of training the militia according to the discipline prescribed by Congress.

17. To exercise exclusive legislation in all cases whatsoever, over such district (not exceeding ten miles square) as may, by cession of particular States, and the acceptance of Congress, become the seat of government of the United States, and to exercise like authority over all places purchased, by the consent of the Legislature of the State in which the same shall be, for the erection of forts, magazines, arsenals, dock-yards, and other needful buildings; and

18. To make all laws which shall be necessary and proper for carrying into execution the foregoing powers, and all other powers vested by this Constitution in the government of the United States, or in any department or office thereof.

[869] SECTION 9.—*Powers Denied the States.*

1. The migration or importation of such persons as any of the States now existing shall think proper to admit, shall not be prohibited by the Congress prior to the year one thousand eight hundred and eight; but a tax or duty may be imposed on such importation not exceeding ten dollars for each person.

2. The privilege of the writ of *habeas corpus* shall not be suspended unless when, in case of rebellion or invasion, the public safety may require it.

3. No bill of attainder, or *ex-post-facto* law, shall be passed.

4. No capitation or other direct tax shall be laid, unless in proportion to the census or enumeration herein before directed to be taken.

5. No tax or duty shall be laid on articles exported from any State.

6. No preference shall be given by any regulation of commerce or revenue to the ports of one State over those of another; nor shall vessels bound to or from one State be obliged to enter, clear, or pay duties in another.

7. No money shall be drawn from the treasury but in consequence of appropriations made by law; and a regular statement and account of the receipts and expenditures of all public money shall be published from time to time.

8. No title of nobility shall be granted by the United States; and no person holding any office of profit or trust under them shall, without the consent of the Congress, accept of any present, emolument, office, or title of any kind whatever, from any king, prince, or foreign state.

[870]   SECTION 10.—*Prohibitions Upon the States.*

1. *Absolute.*—No state shall (1) enter into

any treaty, alliance or confederation; (2) grant letters of marque and reprisal; (3) coin money; (4) emit bills of credit; (5) make any thing but gold and silver coin a tender in payment of debts; (6) pass any bill of attainder, *ex post facto* law, or law impairing the obligation of contracts; or (7) grant any title of nobility.

2. Consent of Congress.—No State shall, without consent of Congress, (1) lay any imposts or duties on imports or exports, except what may be absolutely necessary for executing its inspection laws; and the net produce of all duties and imposts laid by any State on imports or exports shall be for the use of the treasury of the United States, and all such laws shall be subject to the revision and control of the Congress. No State shall, without the consent of the Congress, (2) lay any duty of tonnage, (3) keep troops or ships of war in time of peace, (4) enter into any agreement or compact with another State or with a foreign power, or (5) engage in war unless actually invaded, or in such imminent danger as will not admit of delay.

ARTICLE II.—Executive Department.

[871] SECTION 1.—*The President and Vice-President.*

1. Term of Office.—The executive power shall be vested in a President of the United States of America. He shall hold his office during the term of four years; and together with the Vice-President chosen for the same term, be elected as follows:

2. Election.—Each State shall appoint, in

such manner as the Legislature thereof may direct, a number of electors equal to the whole number of Senators and Representatives to which the State may be entitled in the Congress; but no Senator or Representative, or person holding an office of trust or profit under the United States, shall be appointed an elector.

3. [*This clause provided that the person receiving the highest number of electoral votes should be President, and the person receiving the next highest Vice-President, etc. In 1804, it was annulled and superseded by the XIIth Amendment* (896).]

4. *Time of Election.*—The Congress may determine the time of choosing the electors, and the day on which they shall give their votes, which day shall be the same throughout the United States.

5. *Qualifications.*—No person except (1) a natural born citizen, or a citizen of the United States at the time of the adoption of this Constitution, shall be eligible to the office of President: neither shall any person be eligible to that office who shall not have (2) attained to the age of thirty-five years, and (3) been fourteen years a resident within the United States.

6. *Vacancies; How Filled.*—In case of the removal of the President from office, or of his death, resignation, or inability to discharge the powers and duties of the said office, the same shall devolve on the Vice-President; and the Congress may, by law, provide for the case of removal, death, resignation, or inabil-

ity, both of the President and Vice-President declaring what officer shall then act as President; and such officer shall act accordingly, until the disability be removed or a President shall be elected.

7. *Salary.*—The President shall, at stated times, receive for his services a compensation, which shall neither be increased nor diminished during the period for which he shall have been elected, and he shall not receive within that period any other emolument from the United States, or any of them.

8. *Oath of Office.*—Before he enter on the execution of his office, he shall take the following oath or affirmation:—

"I do solemnly swear (or affirm) that I will faithfully execute the office of President of the United States, and will, to the best of my ability, preserve, protect, and defend the Constitution of the United States."

[872] SECTION 2.—*Powers of the President.*

1. *Commander-in-Chief, etc.*—The President shall be Commander-in-Chief of the army and navy of the United States, and of the militia of the several States, when called into the actual service of the United States. He may require the opinion, in writing, of the principal officer in each of the executive departments, upon any subject relating to the duties of their respective offices; and he shall have power to grant reprieves and pardons for offenses against the United States, except in cases of impeachment.

2. *Treaties and Nominations.*—He shall have

power, by and with the advice and consent of
the Senate, to make treaties, provided two-
thirds of the Senators present concur; and he
shall nominate, and by and with the advice
and consent of the Senate shall appoint ambassadors, other public ministers and consuls,
judges of the Supreme Court, and all other officers of the United States whose appointments are not herein otherwise provided for,
and which shall be established by law. But
the Congress may, by law, vest the appointment of such inferior officers as they may
think proper, in the President alone, in the
courts of law, or in the heads of departments.

3. Vacancies.—The President shall have
power to fill up all vacancies that may happen during the recess of the Senate, by granting commissions which shall expire at the end
of their next session.

[873]   SECTION 3.—*Duties of the President.*

1. He shall, from time to time, give to the
Congress information of the state of the Union, and recommend to their consideration
such measures as he shall judge necessary and
expedient. He may, on extraordinary occa-
sions, convene both houses, or either of them;
and in case of disagreement between them
with respect to the time of adjournment, he
may adjourn them to such time as he shall
think proper. He shall receive ambassadors
and other public ministers. He shall take
care that the laws be faithfully executed; and
shall commission all the officers of the United
States.

[874]   SECTION 4.—*Impeachments.*

The President, Vice-President and all civil officers of the United States, shall be removed from office on impeachment for, and conviction of, treason, bribery, or other high crimes or misdemeanors.

ARTICLE III.—Judicial Department.

[875]   SECTION 1.—*Courts.*

The judicial power of the United States shall be vested in one Supreme Court, and in such inferior courts as Congress may, from time to time, ordain and establish. The judges, both of the supreme and inferior courts, shall hold their offices during good behavior; and shall, at stated times, receive for their services a compensation, which shall not be diminished during their continuance in office.

[876]   SECTION 2.—*Jurisdiction.*

1. Extent.—The judicial power shall extend to all cases in law and equity arising under this Constitution, the laws of the United States and treaties made, or which shall be made under their authority; to all cases affecting ambassadors, other public ministers and consuls; to all cases of admiralty and maritime jurisdiction; to controversies to which the United States shall be a party; to controversies between two or more States; between a State and citizens of another State; between citizens of different States; between citizens of the same State claiming lands under grants of different States and between a State, or the citizens thereof, and foreign

States, citizens or subjects.

2. Ambassadors, etc.—In all cases affecting ambassadors, other public ministers and consuls, and those in which a State shall be a party, the Supreme Court shall have original jurisdiction. In all the other cases before mentioned, the Supreme Court shall have appellate jurisdiction, both as to law and fact, with such exceptions and under such regulations as the Congress may make.

3. Trial of crimes.—The trial of all crimes, except in cases of impeachment, shall be by jury; and such trial shall be held in the State where the said crime shall have been committed; but when not committed within any State, the trial shall be at such place or places as the Congress may by law have directed.

[877]   SECTION 3.—*Treason.*

1. Proof of.—Treason against the United States shall consist only in levying war against them, or in adhering to their enemies, giving them aid and comfort. No person shall be convicted of treason unless on the testimony of two witnesses to the same overt act, or on confession in open court.

2. Punishment.—The Congress shall have power to declare the punishment of treason; but no attainder of treason shall work corruption of blood, or forfeiture, except during the life of the person attained.

ARTICLE IV.—Relations of States.

[878]   SECTION 1.—*State Records.*

Full faith and credit shall be given in each

State to the public acts, records, and judicial proceedings of every other State; and the Congress may, by general laws, prescribe the manner in which such acts, records and proceedings shall be proved, and the effects thereof.

[879] SECTION 2.—*Rights of Citizens, etc.*

1. The citizens of each State shall be entitled to all the privileges and immunities of citizens in the several States.

2. Extradition.—A person charged in any State with treason, felony, or other crime, who shall flee from justice and be found in another State, shall, on demand of the executive authority of the State from which he fled, be delivered up, to be removed to the State having jurisdiction of the crime.

3. An Obsolete Clause Regarding Slavery.— No person held to service or labor in one State, under the laws thereof, escaping into another, shall, in consequence of any law or regulation therein, be discharged from such service or labor, but shall be delivered up on claim of the party to whom such service or labor may be due.

[880] SECTION 3. *New States and Territories.*

1. Admission.—New States may be admitted by the Congress into this Union; but no new State shall be formed or erected within the jurisdiction of any other State; nor any State be formed by the junction of two or more States, or parts of States, without the consent of the Legislatures of the States concerned, as well as of the Congress.

2. Disposition.—The Congress shall have power to dispose of, and make all needful rules and regulations respecting the territory or other property belonging to the United States; and nothing in this Constitution shall be so construed as to prejudice any claims of the United States or of any particular State.

[881] SECTION 4.—*Protection Guaranteed the States.*

The United States shall guarantee to every State in this Union a republican form of government, and shall protect each of them against invasion; and, on application of the Legislature, or of the executive (when the Legislature cannot be convened), against domestic violence.

ARTICLE V.—Amendments.

[882] The Congress, whenever two-thirds of both houses shall deem it necessary, shall propose amendments to this Constitution, or, on the application of the Legislatures of two-thirds of the several States, shall call a convention for proposing amendments, which, in either case, shall be valid to all intents and purposes as part of this Constitution, when ratified by the Legislatures of three-fourths of the several States, or by conventions in three-fourths thereof, as the one or the other mode of ratification may be proposed by Congress; provided that no amendment which

may be made prior to the year one thousand
eight hundred and eight shall in any manner
affect the first and fourth clauses in the ninth
section of the first article; and that no State,
without its consent, shall be deprived of its
equal suffrage in the Senate.

ARTICLE VI.—Public Debt-Supreme Law-Oaths.

[883] *Validity of Debt.*—All debts contract-
ed and engagements entered into before the
adoption of this Constitution shall be as valid against the United States under this Constitution as under the Confederation.

2. Supreme Law.—This Constitution, and
the laws of the United States which shall be
made in pursuance thereof, and all treaties
made, or which shall be made, under the authority of the United States, shall be the supreme law of the land; and the judges in every
State shall be bound thereby, anything in the
Constitution or laws of any State to the con-
trary notwithstanding.

3. Oath; Religious Test.—The Senators and
Representatives before mentioned, and the
members of the several State Legislatures,
and all executive and judicial officers, both
of the United States and of the several States,
shall be bound by oath or affirmation to
support this Constitution; but no religious
test shall ever be required as a qualification
to any office or public trust under the United
States.

ARTICLE VII.—Ratification of Constitution.

[884] The ratification of the conventions of

nine States shall be sufficient for the establishment of this Constitution between the States so ratifying the same.

AMENDMENTS.

[The first ten Amendments were adopted in 1791. The 11th in 1798, the 12th in 1804, the 13th in 1865, the 14th in 1868, and the 15th in 1870.]

I.—*Freedom of Religion, Speech and Press.*

[885] Congress shall make no law respecting an establishment of religion, or prohibiting the free exercise thereof; or abridging the freedom of speech or of the press; or the right of the people peaceably to assemble, and to petition the government for a redress of grievances.—(*1791.*)

II.—*Arms.*

[886] A well regulated militia being necessary to the security of a free State, the right of the people to keep and bear arms shall not be infringed.—(*1791.*)

III.—*Quartering Soldiers.*

[887] No soldier shall, in time of peace, be quartered in any house, without the consent of the owner, nor in time of war, but in a manner to be prescribed by law.—(*1791.*)

IV.—*Search Warrants.*

[888] The right of the people to be secure in their persons, houses, papers and effects, against unreasonable searches and seizures, shall not be violated; and no warrants shall issue but upon probable cause, supported by oath or affirmation, and particularly describing the place to be searched, and the persons

or things to be seized.—(*1791.*)

V.—*Criminal Offenses.*

[889] No person shall be held to answer for a capital or otherwise infamous crime, unless on a presentment or indictment of a grand jury, except in cases arising in the land or naval forces, or in the militia, when in actual service in time of war or public danger; nor shall any person be subject for the same offense to be twice put in jeopardy of life or limb; nor shall be compelled, in any criminal case, to be a witness against himself, nor be deprived of life, liberty or property, without due process of law; nor shall private property be taken for public use without just compensation.—(*1791.*)

VI.—*Criminal Prosecutions.*

[890] In all criminal prosecutions, the accused shall enjoy the right to a speedy and public trial, by an impartial jury of the State and district wherein the crime shall have been committed, which district shall have been previously ascertained by law; and to be informed of the nature and cause of the accusation; to be confronted with the witnesses against him; to have compulsory process for obtaining witnesses in his favor, and to have the assistance of counsel for his defense.—(*1791.*)

VII.—*Trial by Jury.*

[891] In suits at common law, where the value in controversy shall exceed twenty dollars, the right of trial by jury shall be pre-

served; and no fact tried by a jury shall be otherwise re-examined in any court of the United States, than according to the rules of the common law. (*1791.*)

VIII.—*Excessive Punishment.*

[892] Excessive bail shall not be required, nor excessive fines imposed, nor cruel and unusual punishment inflicted.—(*1791.*)

IX.—*Rights Not Named.*

[893] The enumeration in the Constitution of certain rights shall not be construed to deny or disparage others retained by the people.—(*1791.*)

X.—*Powers Reserved.*

[894] The powers not delegated to the United States by the Constitution, nor prohibited to it by the States, are reserved to the States respectively, or to the people.—(*1791.*)

XI.—*Suits Against States.*

[895] The judicial power of the United States shall not be construed to extend to any suit in law or equity, commenced or prosecuted against one of the United States by citizens of another State, or by citizens or subjects of any foreign state.—(*1798.*)

XII.—*Election of President.*

[896] *1.* The electors shall meet in their respective States, and vote by ballot for President and Vice-President, one of whom at least, shall not be an inhabitant of the same State with themselves; they shall name in their ballots the person voted for as Presi-

17

dent, and in distinct ballots the person voted
for as Vice-President; and they shall make
distinct lists of all persons voted for as President, and for all persons voted for as Vice-
President, and of the number of votes for
each; which lists they shall sign and certify,
and transmit sealed to the seat of government of the United States, directed to the
President of the Senate. The President of the
Senate shall, in the presence of the Senate and
House of Representatives, open all of the
certificates, and the votes shall be counted.
The person having the greatest number of
votes for President shall be President, if such
number be a majority of the whole number
of electors appointed; and if no person have
such majority, then from the persons having
the highest number, not exceeding three, on
the list of those voted for as President, the
House of Representatives shall choose immediately, by ballot, the President. But in
choosing the President, the votes shall be
taken by States, the representation from each
State having one vote; a quorum for this
purpose shall consist of a member or members from two-thirds of the States, and a majority of all the States shall be necessary to a
choice. And if the House of Representatives
shall not choose a President, whenever the
right of choice shall devolve upon them, before the fourth day of March next following,
then the Vice-President shall act as President,
as in case of death or other constitutional
disability of the President.

2. Vice-President.—The person having the greatest number of votes as Vice-President shall be the Vice-President, if such number be a majority of the whole number of electors appointed; and if no person have a majority, then from the two highest numbers on the list the Senate shall choose the Vice-President; a quorum for the purpose shall consist of two-thirds of the whole number of Senators, and a majority of the whole number shall be necessary to a choice.

3. Eligibility.—But no person constitutionally ineligible to the office of President shall be eligible to that of Vice-President of the United States.—(*1804.*)

XIII.—*Slavery.*

[897] *1.* Neither slavery nor involuntary servitude, except as a punishment for crime, whereof the party shall have been duly convicted, shall exist within the United States, or any place subject to their jurisdiction.

2. Congress shall have power to enforce this article by appropriate legislation.—(*1865.*)

XIV.—*Civil Rights.*

[898] *1. Civil Rights.*—All persons born or naturalized in the United States and subject to the jurisdiction thereof, are citizens of the United States and of the State wherein they reside. No State shall make or enforce any law which shall abridge the privileges or immunities of the citizens of the United States; nor shall any State deprive any person of life, liberty or property, without due pro-

cess of law; nor deny to any person within its jurisdiction the equal protection of the laws.

2. Apportionment of Representatives.—Representatives shall be apportioned among the several States according to their respective numbers, counting the whole number of persons in each State, excluding Indians not taxed. But when the right to vote at any election for the choice of electors for President and Vice-President of the United States, Representatives in Congress, the executive and judicial officers of a State, or the members of the Legislature thereof, is denied to any of the male inhabitants of such State, being twenty-one years of age, and a citizen of the United States, or in any way abridged, except for participation in rebellion or other crime, the basis of representation therein shall be reduced in the proportion which the number of such male persons shall bear to the whole number of male citizens twenty-one years of age in such State.

3. Political Disabilities.—No person shall be a Senator or Representative in Congress, or elector of President and Vice-President, or hold any office, civil or military, under the United States, or under any State, who having previously taken an oath as a member of Congress, or as an officer of the United States, or as a member of any State Legislature, or as an executive or judicial officer of any State, to support the Constitution of the United States, shall have engaged in insurrection or rebellion against the same, or giv-

en aid or comfort to the enemies thereof.
But Congress may, by a two-thirds vote of
each house, remove such disability.

4. Public Debt.—The validity of the public
debt of the United States authorized by law,
including debts incurred for payment of pensions and bounties for services in suppressing
insurrection or rebellion, shall not be questioned. But neither the United States nor
any State shall assume or pay any debt or
obligation incurred in aid of insurrection or
rebellion against the United States, or any
claim for the loss or emancipation of any slave;
but all such debts, obligations and claims
shall be held illegal and void.

5. Enforcement.—The Congress shall have
power to enforce, by appropriate legislation,
the provsions of this article.—(*1868.*)

XV.—*Suffrage.*

[899] *1.* The right of the citizens of the
United States to vote shall not be denied or
abridged by the United States or by any State
on account of race, color, or previous condition of servitude.   ~

2. Enforcement.—Congress shall have power
to enforce, by appropriate legislation, the
provisions of this article. (*1870.*)

WEST VIRGINIA.

900. Adjutant-General.—Appointed by Governor. Term, four years. Salary, $1,200. Has rank of colonel, with brevet rank of brigadier general. Is *ex-officio* quarter-master-general, and superintendent of weights and measures. Executes all lawful orders of the Governor. Delivers the Governor's orders to the militia, and carries out all his orders concerning it. Also performs the regular duties of his other offices.

901. Attorney-General.—Elected. Term, four years. Salary, $1,300, and fees. Must be twenty-five years of age and a citizen five years. Need not reside at capital. Commissioned by Governor. Is counsel for the State. Gives legal advice to State officers. Passes on validity of bonds. Removes unlawful bridges across navigable rivers.

902. Auditor.—Elected. Term, four years. Salary, $2,000, and fees. Must reside at capital. Keeps account of all appropriations and expenditures. Examines claims against the State, and issues warrants on the treasurer. Audits claims on sheriffs and other officers. Furnishes forms for assessors, and instructs them. Keeps records of land and other property. Bond, $20,000.

903. Board of Agriculture.—Appointed by Governor. Number, five—one from each Congressional District, and one at large. Term, four years. Compensation, $4 per day when engaged, and traveling expenses. Practical farmers engaged in the business. Promotes agricultural interests by holding institutes, sending out agricultural documents, etc. Elects Secretary, with office at capital, whose salary cannot exceed $1,000, and traveling expenses.

904. Board of Dental Examiners.—Appointed by Governor. Number, five. Term, five years. Compensation, fees. Examine applicants, and issue licenses to practice dentistry.

905. Board of Directors W. Va. Asylum for Incurables.—Appointed by Governor with consent of Senate. Number, eight—four men and four women—one of each appointed every two years. Compensation, fixed by Board of Public Works, not more than $3 per day when employed, and ten cents mileage to and from asylum. Has general control of asylum.

906. Board of Directors Hospital for Insane at Weston.—Appointed by Governor with consent of Senate. Number, nine. Term, six years. Compensation, $4 per day when employed, and expenses. Not more than one Director from any one county. Chooses a member president every two years. Has general control of the affairs of the institution.

907. Board of Directors Second Hospital for Insane at Spencer.—Same provisions as for board for hospital at Weston.

**908. Board of Directors W. Va. Industrial
Home for Girls.**—Appointed by Governor with
consent of Senate. Number, six—three men
and three women—one of each appointed every two years. Term, six years. Compensation, $4 per day when employed, and expenses. Has general control of the home.

**909. Board of Directors W. Va. Reform
School.**—Appointed by Governor with consent
of Senate. Number, six—not more than four of
same politics. Term, six years. Not more
than two from same county. Chooses a member president every two years. Compensation,
$4 per day when employed, and expenses.
Has general control of the business of the
school.

910. Board of Directors Penitentiary.—Appointed by Governor with consent of Senate.
Number, five—one from Marshall County and
not more than one from any other one county. Compensation, four dollars per day
when employed, and expenses. Has general
control of penitentiary.

911. Board of Pardons or Advisory Board.—
Term, four years. Number, two—one from each
of the two great political parties. Appointed
by the Governor. Compensation, $4 per day;
no mileage, but reasonable expenses not exceeding $600 per year. Meeting, the first Tuesday in April, July and October, of each year,
at Moundsville. Clerk of penitentiary acts as
clerk of the Board. Duties, to consider applications for pardons, commutations and re-

prieves, and to make written recommendations to the Governor as to granting or refusing the same. Governor may remove
members and fill vacancies.

912. Board of Public Works.—Composed of
Governor, Treasurer, State Superintendent of
Free Schools, Auditor, and Attorney-General.
No extra compensation. Secretary of State
ex-officio secretary of board. Assesses railroad property, has charge of all internal improvements, designates banks to be state de-
positories, appoints Commissioners of Pharmacy, Board of Dental Examiners, and Commissioner of Immigration.

**913. Board of Regents Bluefield Colored Insti-
tute.**—Appointed by Governor, to serve at his
will. One from each Congressional District,
and State Superintendent *ex-officio* member—
five in all. Compensation, $4 per day
when employed. Duties same as in (918).

**914. Board of Regents Preparatory Branch
W. Va. University at Montgomery.**—Composed
of University regents and State Superintendent of Free Schools, who is *ex-officio* member—ten in all. Duties same as in (918).

**915. Board of Regents W. Va. Colored Insti-
tute.**—Appointed by Governor to serve at his
will. Number, five. Not more than three of
same politics. Compensation, $4 per
day when employed, and expenses. Duties same as in (918).

916. Board of Regents State Normal Schools.—
Appointed by the Governor. Number, five—
one from each Congressional District, and

State Superintendent *ex-officio* member.
Term, four years. Compensation, $4
per day when employed, and expenses.
Duties same as in (918).

**917. Board of Regents W. Va. Schools for
Deaf and Blind.**—Appointed by Governor.
Number, seven—not more than two from any
one Congressional District. Compensation,
$4 per day when employed, and expenses.
Has general control of the business of the
school.

918. Board of Regents of W. Va. University.—
Appointed by Governor with consent of Senate. Number, nine. Compensation, $4 per day
when employed, and expenses. No two from
same Senatorial District. Not more than five
of the same political party. Appoints instructors; has charge of buildings and funds,
receives gifts, and transacts the general business of the university.

919. Board of School Fund.—Composed of
Governor (*ex-officio* President), Auditor (*ex-officio* Secretary*), State Superintendent of
Free Schools, and Treasurer. Has control of
permanent school fund. Meets in Auditor's
office.

920. Commissioner of Immigration.—Appointed by Board of Public works. Term, at
pleasure of board. Salary and duties fixed by
board. Object, to encourage immigration of
proper persons.

921. Commissioner of Labor.—Appointed by
Governor. Term, four years. Salary, $1,200;
assistant, $800. Collects and compiles la-

bor and industrial statistics. Must visit principal factories and workshops at least once a year.

922. Commissioners of Pharmacy.—Appointed by the Board of Public Works. Number, four —one from each Congressional District. Compensation, fees. Must have five year's residence in State; also five year's experience. Examine applicants and grant licenses to pharmacists.

923. Commissioners of Public Printing.—Number, three—Auditor, Treasurer and State Superintendent of Free Schools. Contracts for State printing and binding, and for stationery for the use of the State. No extra Compensation.

924. Congressional Districts.—*First*, Hancock, Brooke, Ohio, Marshall, Wetzel, Tyler, Doddridge, Harrison, Gilmer, Lewis and Braxton.

Second, Monongalia, Marion, Preston, Taylor, Barbour, Randolph, Tucker, Pendleton, Hardy, Mineral, Hampshire, Grant, Morgan, Jefferson and Berkeley.

Third, Logan, Wyoming, McDowell, Mercer, Raleigh, Boone, Kanawha, Fayette, Clay, Nicholas, Greenbrier, Monroe, Summers, Webster, Pocahontas, Upshur and Mingo.

Fourth, Pleasants, Wood, Ritchie, Wirt, Calhoun, Jackson, Roane, Mason, Putnam, Cabell, Lincoln and Wayne.

925. Days of Grace.—Days of grace are not allowed on any negotiable paper made after May 23, 1899, unless otherwise provided in such instrument.

926. Delegates.—Elected. Number, seventy one. Term, two years. `Compensation, $4 per day, and 10 cents mileage in going to, and returning from the capital. Privileged from arrest. Residence required in district. Effect of removal from county or delegate district, beginning of term, and freedom in debate, the same as in the case of Senators (938).

927. Game and Fish Warden.—Appointed by Governor. Term, four years. Salary, all fines up to $1,200, and 20 per cent. of all over that amount; also mileage. Prosecutes offenders against game and fish laws.

928. Governor.—Chief executive. Elected. Term, four years. Salary, $2,700. Cannot serve two successive terms. Must be 30 years of age at beginning of term, and a citizen of the State five years, at election. Commander-in-Chief of the State militia. Approves or vetoes bills. Appoints certain officers with consent of Senate. May remove those whom he appoints. Must reside at capital. Can hold no other office during his term. May convene Legislature in extra session; *must* do so on written application of three-fifth of the members elected to each house. Approves State contracts for printing, etc. Gives information and recommendations to Legislature by message. Temporarily fills vacancies in elective State offices. May, for safety, convene Legislature at another place than the capital. May call out militia to enforce law, suppress insurrection and repel invasion. Has pardoning, commuting and reprieving power. May require information in writing under oath from subordinate executive officers. Vacancy in office of Governor filled in order (*1*) by President of Senate; or (*2*) by Speaker of House; or, (*3*) by person chosen by joint session of the Legislature. If the vacancy occurs before the end of third year of term, it is filled by special election.

929. Judges of Circuit Courts.—Elected. Number, fourteen. Term, eight years. Salary, $1,800, and ten cents mileage. Can hold no other office during term. Cannot practice law. All elected at same time. Qualifications, same as for Governor (**928**).

930. Judges of Supreme Court of Appeals.—Elected. Number, four. Term, twelve years. Salary, $2,200, and ten cents mileage. Commissioned by Governor. Can hold no other office during his term. Cannot practice law. Two elected every six years. Qualifications same as for Governor (**928**).

931. Judicial Circuits.—*First*, Hancock, Brooke, Ohio, Marshall. *Two Judges.*

Second, Harrison, Marion, Monongalia.

Third, Barbour, Preston, Randolph, Taylor, Tucker.

Fourth, Doddridge, Ritchie, Tyler, Wetzel.

Fifth, Pleasants, Wirt, Wood.

Sixth, Calhoun, Clay, Gilmer, Jackson, Roane.

Seventh, Kanawha, Mason, Putnam.

Eighth, Cabell, Lincoln, Logan, Mingo, Wayne.

Ninth, Boone, McDowell, Mercer, Raleigh, Wyoming,

. *Tenth*, Fayette, Greenbrier, Monroe, Pocahontas, Summers.

Eleventh, Braxton, Lewis, Nicholas, Upshur, Webster.

Twelfth, Grant, Hampshire, Hardy, Mineral, Pendleton.

Thirteenth, Berkley, Jefferson, Morgan.

. **932. Legal Holidays.**—The following are, by statute, made legal holidays in the State:

New Year's Day, January 1st.

Washington's Birth Day, February 22nd.

Independence Day, July 4th.

Memorial Day, May 30th.

Christmas Day, December 25th.

Labor Day, the first Monday in September.

National and State election days.

All days appointed by the Governor or President as days of thanksgiving or for the general cessation of business.

If a legal holiday falls on Sunday, then the succeeding Monday is a legal holiday.—*Ch. 13, Acts 1899.*

933. Mine Inspectors.—Appointed by Governor. Term, four years. Four districts—one inspector in each. Also, one chief mine inspector. Salaries; chief, $1,500; inspectors $1,000. Must have six year's experience as miners. Visit all mines in district for inspection at least once every three months. $300 each per year for expenses. Bond, $2,000.

934. Notaries Public.—Appointed and commissioned by Governor. Compensation, fees.

Hold office during good behavior. As many as Governor thinks proper to appoint. Can act only in the county for which appointed. Take acknowledgment of deeds and other writings. Administer oaths. Protest commercial paper. Are conservators of the peace. Bond, $250 to $1,000.

935. Protest.—Papers falling due on a Sunday or on a legal holiday, are payable and may be protested on the succeeding day.

Papers falling due on a Saturday, are due and payable before 12 o'clock, noon, of that day.

936. Secretary of State.—Appointed by Governor. Term, four years. Salary $1,000, and fees. Bond, $10,000. Besides usual oath, must swear to keep secret what the Governor requires him to conceal. Keeper of State Seals. Preserves journal of executive proceedings, State records and all executive papers. Issues charters. Distributes reports and copies of law. Aids Governor as required by him. Has general clerical duties.

937. Senatorial Districts.—*First*, Hancock, Brooke, Ohio.

Second, Marshall, Wetzel, Marion.

Third, Tyler, Ritchie, Doddridge, Harrison.

Fourth, Pleasants, Wood, Wirt, Calhoun, Gilmer.

Fifth, Jackson, Roane, Mason.

Sixth, Cabell, Wayne, Putnam.

Seventh, Logan, Lincoln, Wyoming, McDowell, Mercer, Raleigh, Mingo.

Eighth, Greenbrier, Monroe, Summers, Fayette, Pocahontas.

Ninth, Kanawha, Nicholas. Braxton, Clay, Boone.

Tenth, Randolph, Lewis, Upshur, Barbour, Webster.

Eleventh, Preston, Monongalia, Taylor.

Twelfth, Hampshire, Hardy, Grant, Mineral, Pendleton, Tucker.

Thirteenth, Jefferson, Berkley, Morgan.

938. State Senators.—Elected. Number, twenty-six. Term, four years. Compensation, $4 per day during session, and ten cents mileage to and from the capital. Must be twenty-five years of age and citizen five years. No two from same county. Divided into two classes—one from each district elected every two years. Privileged from arrest during session and ten days before and after, except for treason, felony and breach of peace. Removal from district vacates office. Must reside in district one year before election. Term begins first of December after election. Can not, except in the Senate, be questioned for words spoken in debate.

939. State Bank Examiner.—Appointed by Governor. Term, four years. Salary $700; also $15 to be paid by each bank examined. Must be skilled in book-keeping and banking. Must personally examine each State (not national) bank, and, before Sept. 30th of each year, send to Auditor detailed report of condition and financial standing of same.

940. State Board of Examiners.—Appointed by the State Superintendent of Free Schools.

Number, four—one from each Congressional District. Term, four years. Compensation, $5 per day when employed, and 6 cents mileage. Examines teachers and issues State Certificates. Compensation must be paid by fees received. State Superintendent countersigns certificates.

941. State Board of Embalmers.—Term, four years. Number, eight—two from each Congressional District. Compensation, $2 per meeting and expenses. Secretary, $100 per year. Meet once a year, with special sessions. Duties, to examine and license embalmers, and to keep a register of the same. Elect a President, Secretary and Treasurer from their number.

942. State Board of Health.—Appointed by Governor. Number, eight—two from each Congressional District. Compensation, $4 per day when employed, and expenses. Graduate physicians of twelve years' experience. Term, four years. May be removed by Governor. Two appointed every second year. Every two years, elects President and Secretary from members. Secretary's salary not more than $500, with not more than $100 for traveling expenses. Board examines applicants and issues licenses to practice medicine. Also has general supervision of the health affairs of the State.

943. State Librarian.—Appointed by Governor. Term, four years. Salary, $1,000. Has charge of state library.

944. State School Fund.—The P E R M A N E N T
18

OR IRREDUCIBLE SCHOOL FUND is made up from the following sources as provided in the Constitution:

1. The proceeds of forfeited, delinquent, waste and unappropriated lands.

2. Grants, devises, bequests made to the State, unless given for some specific purpose.

3. The State's share of the Literary Fund of Virginia.

4. Any money, stocks or property received from Virginia for educational purposes.

5. Proceeds of estates of persons who may die without leaving a will or heir.

6. Proceeds of any taxes levied on the revenues of any corporations.

7. Moneys paid for exemption from military duty.

8. Any appropriations made by the Legislature for the fund.

9. Any part of the interest remaining unexpended at the close of any fiscal year.

The Fund now amounts to over $800,000, and is invested in interest-bearing securities.

Only the interest can be annually expended for school purposes.

Board of the School Fund, (919).

The GENERAL SCHOOL FUND, provided for by statute, is made up of—

1. A State tax of ten cents on each $100 valuation.

2. The net proceeds of fines.

3. Capitation tax.

4. Annual interest on the Permanent School Fund.

This Fund is apportioned among the school districts of the State according to the school enumeration.

945. State Superintendent of Free Schools.— Elected. Term, four years. Salary, $1,500. Must reside at capital. Has general supervision of free schools. Has supervision of County Superintendents. Distributes school blanks, copies of school law, etc. Supervises institutes. Collects statistics.

946. Treasurer.—Elected. Term, four years. Salary, $1,400. Must reside at the capital. Keeps account of all appropriations and moneys turned into the treasury; also of all disbursements. Issues checks on treasury on the warrants of Auditor. Bond, $25,000.

947. Vaccine Agents.—Appointed by Governor. Term, four years. Salary, $50. One must reside at Charleston, one at Martinsburg, and one at Wheeling. Must furnish to citizens on application, free of charge, vaccine matter and directions for use.

948. Warden of Penitentiary.—Appointed by Governor with consent of Senate. Term, four years. Salary, not over $1,500. Executive officer of Penitentiary under Board of Directors. Bond, $10,000.

949. West Virginia Courts.—The system comprises the following courts in the order given, beginning with the highest:

SUPREME COURT OF APPEALS.—The highest court of the State. Consists of four judges, three being a quorum. It holds three sessions every year—one at Charleston, commencing the 2nd Wednesday in January; one at Wheeling, commencing the 1st Wednesday in June; and one in Charlestown, commencing the 1st Wednesday in September.

Original jurisdiction, in cases of *habeas corpus*, *mandamus*, and prohibition.

Appellate jurisdiction, in civil cases where the amount in controversy exclusive of cost, exceeds $100; in land and will cases; in cases involving constitutional questions; in criminal cases; in cases of *quo warranto*, *habeas corpus*, *mandamus*, *certiorari* and prohibition; in a few other cases prescribed by the constitution; and such other appellate jurisdiction as may be prescribed by law.

If a vacancy occurs within two years or more of the close of the term, the Governor issues *writs of election* to fill such vacancy at the next general election for the remainder of the term, and fills such vacancy until a judge is elected and qualified.

But if the unexpired time be less than two years, the Governor fills it by appointment.

The Governor, or President of said court, may convene same to revise a case.

The Attorney General acts as Court Reporter. *Supreme Judges*, (930).

CIRCUIT COURT.—It must hold at least three sessions in each County every year at times prescribed by law.

It has *original* jurisdiction in all cases when the amount in controversy, exclusive of interest, exceeds $50; in all cases of *habeas corpus*, *mandamus*, *quo warranto*, and prohibition;

in all cases of equity, and all crimes and misdemeanors.

Its *appellate* jurisdiction extends to all cases, civil and criminal, where an appeal, writ of error or supersedeas may be allowed to the judgment or proceedings of any inferior tribunal. It may have other jurisdiction, supervisory, original, appellate or concurrent, as prescribed by law.

Special terms may be called by the judge, by a warrant directed to the clerk.

Circuit Judges, (929). *Circuit Clerk*, (952).

COUNTY COURT.—Composed of three commissioners—any two of whom constitute a quorum. It has the custody of deeds and other papers presented for record in the respective counties.

Its jurisdiction extends to matters of probate, the appointment and qualification of personal representatives, guardians, committees, curators, and the settlement of their accounts; and to all matters relating to apprentices, etc.

It has power to issue license for the sale of intoxicating liquors.

It holds four regular sessions each year at times fixed by said court, and may hold special sessions whenever the public interests require it. *Commissioners*, (956). *Clerk*, (953).

JUSTICE'S COURT.—The lowest court of the State. It has only original jurisdiction.

Its jurisdiction extends to cases of debt, detinue and trover, if the amount claimed, exclusive of interest, does not exceed $300; and to misdemeanors.

It must have a jury of six, if demanded by either party in a suit, when the amount in controversy exceeds $20.

Cases may be appealed to the Circuit Court when the amount in controversy exceeds $15 exclusive of interest and costs, or the case involves the freedom of a person, the validity of a law, or an ordinance of any coporation, or the right of a corporation to levy tolls or taxes. *Justices.* (970).

CRIMINAL COURTS.— Special courts created by particular legislative acts, for the trial of · criminal cases in sections where the regular courts are over-crowded with work.

THE COUNTY.

950. Agent of County Infirmary.—Appointed by County Court and serves at its pleasure. Compensation, fixed by said Court. Superintends affairs of Infirmary. Bond fixed by court.

951. Assesssor.—One in each county; in certain counties, two. Elected. Term, four years. Salary, $200 to $350 (a few counties may pay more); also fees and commissions. Duty, to list the taxable property and polls of his disrict; to issue certificates for State license, and to register births and deaths for the preceding year. Bond, $2,000 to $5,000.

952. Clerk of Circuit Court.—Elected. Term, six years. Salary, $200 to $1200 according to county; also fees. Records proceedings and preserves all records and papers of court. Prepares bonds given before the court. Furnishes copies of records. Issues subpoenas, processes, orders of affairs, etc. Bond, $3,000 to $10,000.

953. Clerk of County Court.—Elected. Term, six years. Salary, $200 to $600; also fees. Records proceedings of court and does clerical work. Records deeds and other papers. Probates wills. Issues marriage licenses, etc., etc. Preserves county records and papers. Bond, $3,000 to $10,000.

954. Commissioners in Chancery.—Appointed by Circuit Court. Term, at its pleasure. Number, not more than four. Compensation, fees. Examine and report on accounts and matters referred to them by the court.

955. Commissioners of Accounts.—Appointed by County Court. Number, not more than four. Compensation, fees. Supervise fiduciaries (847), examine their accounts and settle with them.

956. Commissioners of County Court.—Elected. Number, three. Term, six years—one elected every two years. Compensation, $2 per day when employed. No two from same district. Two a quorum. Annually elect one of their number President; they may administer oaths, take affidavits or depositions, acknowledgments of deeds, etc., and are conservators of the peace. They levy county taxes and pay county expenses. Appoint road surveyors, over-seers of the poor, coro-

ners, commissioners of accounts, election officers, guardians, administrators, etc. Have
charge of county buildings, roads, bridges fer-
ries, district boundary lines, county infirm-
aries, the probating of wills and the recording
of deeds and other papers, the counting and
certifying election returns, etc., etc. Four
regular sessions per year. Extra sessions at
pleasure of court.

957. Commissioner of School Lands.—Appointed by Circuit Court. Term, at its pleasure. Compensation, fees and commissions.
Sells public school lands—lands purchased by
the State for taxes, and waste and unappropriated lands. Bond, at least $5,000.

958. Coroner.—Appointed by County Court
to serve during its pleasure. Compensation,
fees. Inquires into mysterious deaths. Can
issue warrant for person shown to be guilty
in a case. Justice acts if coroner cannot.

959. County Board of Examiners.—Nominated by the County Superintendent of Free
Schools and chosen by Presidents of Boards
of Education. Two members, and County
Superintendent, who is *ex-officio* member and
President of Board. Term, two years. Compensation, $3 per day when employed. Paid
out of fees. Holds two or more examinations of teachers each year.

960. County Superintendent of Free Schools.
—Elected. Term, four years. Salary, for 50
schools, $150; 51 to 75 schools, $200; 76 to 100
schools, $250; over 100 schools, $300. Paid
out of general school fund. Visits schools.

Advises teachers. Distributes blanks, etc. Decides appeals from Boards of Education. Approves plans for school houses. Reports to sheriff amount of school fund. Arranges for, and assists in, holding teachers' institutes. Reports statistics to State Superintendent. Tie vote for the office decided by Presidents of Boards of Education, who select one of those having most votes to serve. Vacancies also filled by the Presidents. Helps examine teachers. Term begins July first. Bond, $500.

961. General Provisions.—*Residence*. All county officers except Prosecuting Attorney must reside in the county.

Removal.—Clerk of Circuit Court, prosecuting attorney, sheriff, surveyor of lands, and county commissioners are removed by Circuit Court.

Clerk of County Court, superintendent of free schools, assessors, justices and constables are removed by either Circuit Court or County Court.

Oath.—All officers are sworn.

Official Bonds.—Bonds of all officers elected, approved by County Court, except that of circuit clerk, which is approved by Circuit Court; and all are filed in the county clerk's office, except that of county clerk, which is filed in the circuit clerk's office.

Bonds of officers appointed by courts are approved by said courts and filed in their respective offices.

962. Jury Commissioners.—Appointed by Circuit Court. Number, two. Term, four years. Paid $2 per day when employed. Of opposite politics. Annually, and when required by court, prepare jury list of not fewer than one hundred names, place same on separate ballots in a box, and draw juries therefrom when needed. Court may remove, and fill vacancy.

963. Local Board of Health.—Two citizens and one physician nominated by County Court and appointed by State Board of Health, to serve two years with President of County Court and prosecuting attorney. Physician paid salary by court, and citizens paid expenses.. Physician executive officer of Board. Look after sanitary affairs of county. Subject to State Board's orders.

964. Prosecuting Attorney.—Elected. Term, four years. Salary, from $200 to $4,000, according to county; also fees. County prosecutor. Gives legal advice to county officers. Must defend or prosecute any suit in which the county or a district is a party.

865. School Book Board.—Composed of the County Superintendent, who is *ex officio* secretary, and eight others appointed by the County Court, at least four of whom must be freeholders not teachers, and at least three active teachers, but not more than five of the same politics. Elects a member President. Contracts for school books for five years, and fixes retail price not exceeding twenty-five per cent. advance on net contract price. Compensation, $2 per day when employed.

966. Sheriff.—Elected. Term, four years. Salary, from $200 to $500 according to county; also commissions and fees. Executive officer of county. Serves judicial writs and processes. Collects taxes and pays county and district orders as county treasurer. Attends Circuit and County Courts as executive officer. Is *ex officio* jailer with power to appoint a substitute. Cannot practice law. Cannot serve two consecutive terms. Can hold no other office for one year after expiration of term. Bond, $20,000 to $150,000.

967. Surveyor of Lands.—Elected. Term, four years. Compensation, fees. Surveys lands on order of any court. Reports waste and unappropriated lands to Circuit Court. Bond, $1,000 to $3,000.

THE DISTRICT.

968. Board of Education.—Elected. Composed of President and two Commissioners. Term, four years. Compensation, $1.50 per day for six days each year. Fixes teachers' salaries. Lays district school levy. Appoints trustees. Locates school houses, etc. Elects secretary who is paid $25 per year.

969. Constable.—Elected. Number, one for each justice. Term, four years. Compensation, fees. Serves summonses, subpoenas, etc., and makes arrests. Has jurisdiction throughout the county.

970. Justice of the Peace.—Elected. Number, two if district has population of more than 1,200; otherwise, one. Term, four years.

Compensation, fees. Civil jurisdiction extends to $300. Issues warrants and subpoenas. Takes acknowledgments, depositions and affidavits. Tries misdemeanors, etc., etc. Has jurisdiction throughout the county.

971. Overseer of Poor.—Appointed by County Court. Term, two years. One in each district. Compensation, not more than $1.50 per day when employed. Assists in caring for the poor.

972. School Trustees.—Appoined by Board of Education. Number, three in each sub-district. Term, three years—one appointed each year. No compensation. Hire teacher; certify time taught; contract for fuel and care of house, etc.

973. Surveyors of Roads.—Appointed by County Court. Number, fixed by court. Term, two years. Compensation, from one dollar to one dollar and fifty cents per day, as fixed by court. Keep roads in their respective precincts in order.

INDEX

Note—Except in a few cases, references are here made only to sub-topics. See Note II, page 7. References below are to pages.

ERRATA.

88, 2, *1*—For	"first,"	read	first.
" " *2*—	" "notority,"	"	notoriety.
106, 2.—	" "govenor,"	"	governor.
145, 5,—	" "juridictions,"	"	jurisdiction.
147, 1.—	" "citlzens,"	"	citizens.
297, 3,—	" **"339,"**	"	**610.**
380, 1.—	" "offiice,"	"	office.
383, 1,—	" "a new trial,"	"	a trial.
397, 7,—	" "eletors,"	"	electors.
414, 1,—	" "sighed,"	"	signed.
610, 1,—	" "1887,"	"	1787.
710, 1,—For	"Righ"	read	Right.
836, 10,—	" "cndidates"	"	candidates.
857, 1,—	" "isstrument,"	"	instrument.

340, 2.—There are now 22 Federal Circuit Judges, the 2nd, 7th, 8th and 9th Circuits having three Judges each, with two in each of the other Circuits.

184, 2, and **146**, 11.—U. S. Commissioners are now appointed by U. S. District Courts for a term of four years.

www.ingramcontent.com/pod-product-compliance
Lightning Source LLC
Chambersburg PA
CBHW030345270326
41926CB00009B/964